In *Kawaii Sweet World*, YouTube sensation Rachel Fong teaches you how to bake super-easy treats that are just as fun to make as they are to eat. Whether you're a cookie rookie or a piping pro, you'll find tips on all the basics, from whipping up the best buttercream to using a turntable to decorate—but this is no ordinary baking book. Why have a plain layer cake when you could have a cuddly corgi cake? These 75 totally original recipes include chocolate cupcakes that transform into snuggly koalas, cake pops that are twinkly-eyed narwhals, lemon cookies that turn into emojis, and cream puffs that become little pink pigs. With *Kawaii Sweet World* cookbook, the fun is baked right in.

KAWAII

SWEET WORLD

KAWAII
SWEET WORLD

75 YUMMY RECIPES FOR BAKING
THAT'S (ALMOST) TOO CUTE TO EAT

RACHEL FONG

PHOTOGRAPHS BY ANDRIA LO

CLARKSON POTTER/PUBLISHERS

NEW YORK

TO MY FAMILY.
Thank you for
making life so
much sweeter.

CONTENTS

INTRODUCTION

There is no better job in the world than making cute desserts for a living. Well, except maybe that of my friends and family, whose part-time job is now eating cute desserts. I'm lucky enough to have the former job, and I get to dream up and create whatever my sweets-loving heart desires every single week! I am the self-taught baker (and college student) behind the YouTube channel "Kawaii Sweet World." I've been posting videos and sharing my love of baking since I was twelve years old, and I'm thrilled to now put some of my favorite recipes into a cookbook for fellow avid bakers to enjoy at home.

It would be an understatement to say I have a sweet tooth. I have a big, unmanageable, insatiable, and overenthusiastic sweet tooth. You know how some people have a slice of chocolate cake and hit a point where they say, "Wow, that was delicious, but I don't think I can have another bite." I just never hit that point. I think I have a second stomach for dessert. Couple that with a passion for baking, and you have a recipe for a baking enthusiast!

My mom, who loves all things creative, taught me to bake when I was very young. My childhood was full of weekend trips to Michaels, creating clay charms beside her as she made jewelry, and, best of all, *lots* of baking. I even used to pretend we were on a cooking show together as we whipped up the latest recipe we'd earmarked in a magazine.

As I was honing my baking skills, I became increasingly interested in the kawaii design style and culture. At the time, I just knew that I loved Hello Kitty and cute stationery decorated with smiling cakes and cupcakes. I had no idea there was a term to describe the style that I adored so much. Then one night, my family took me to San Francisco's Japantown for dinner, and there I encountered the full scope of kawaii culture. "Sensory overload" would be an understatement—it was heaven! The stores were packed with adorable plushies, stationery, purses, T-shirts, and more, all decorated in the kawaii manner, and my heart felt like it was physically aching from the cuteness. One of the notebooks I bought that day featured a bear holding a smiling piece of cake, and it had the phrase "kawaii desserts" written at the top. Curious about this new word, I went home and googled "kawaii desserts" and up popped hundreds of colorful images featuring the cutest designs and graphics I had ever seen. Armed with the correct search term, I was then able to search for "kawaii notebook," "kawaii plush," "kawaii cake," "kawaii desserts," and so on into endless permutations. My elementary-school mind was overwhelmed—but in the best, most excited way possible!

This discovery gave me lots of inspiration for new kawaii crafting and baking projects. I had previously focused only on baking desserts, not on decorating them, but now I was compelled to re-create some of the adorable treats I saw online. The first kawaii treat I baked was a vanilla cake shaped like a cloud with a smiling face. While it was a little rough around the edges (literally—I hadn't yet mastered cake carving!), I loved the process of decorating and customizing it. So, I started revisiting my favorite recipes and putting kawaii twists on them. Whether it was adding bear ears to chocolate chip cookies or arranging sprinkles into a happy face on a cake, I had a blast "kawaii-fying" desserts in simple ways.

And that brings me to the next chapter in my life: YouTube. When I was an awkward middle schooler with a love for making kawaii things, I discovered a crafting contest that was hosted on YouTube. It required a video entry, so I hit "record" and uploaded away! This was big for me: Growing up, I had always been incredibly shy and reserved. Putting myself out there where *anyone* could click, comment, or dislike was terrifying.

And I didn't even win the contest! Bummer, but I got a handful of requests to post tutorials on my crafts. Being a twelve-year-old with a healthy amount of free time, I went for it. I started my own channel, and "Kawaii Sweet World" was born, though at the time, I didn't feature any desserts at all.

At about the same time, I found a small community on YouTube of other people (mostly girls my age) who loved making kawaii polymer clay charms. I got to know them better, along with my own subscribers, and I realized I finally found my little online niche. These were my people! They understood my inexplicable obsession with making cute crafts in a way that my school friends didn't necessarily relate to as much. About a year into my channel, I started featuring some of my favorite recipes as well. I figured I was already baking the desserts for fun, so why not share them with my community? I got an amazing response to the kawaii baked goods. There were very few people doing cake and dessert decorating on YouTube at the time, and no one I knew of who specialized in kawaii baking. So, I created a kawaii niche within a baking and crafting niche, and I loved my little online world.

As I continued posting more videos, my little corner of the internet soon grew into the size of a whole room, and then a house, and suddenly we filled up a whole football stadium when I hit 100,000 subscribers! There was never one particularly big viral hit that helped my channel grow. Rather, I just kept creating more desserts and crafts, all inspired by my love for kawaii things, and I realized more people shared my passion than I ever thought was possible. "Kawaii Sweet World" now has over 2 million followers across social media, and I'm so grateful and happy to have found so many people who love making cute things as much as I do! Nothing was (and still is) more rewarding to me than seeing the photos fans send me of their own re-creations of the treats I feature on my channel.

Beyond my creative side, I will admit that I am a huge nerd. I'm currently a student at Stanford University, where I am studying mechanical engineering. I know, it's a hard-left turn from baking kawaii desserts, but it just goes to show that baking really is for everyone. The combination of being creative with "Kawaii Sweet World" and indulging the nerd in me at school creates a happy balance in my life.

To me, "Kawaii Sweet World" is about so much more than the fun creations I get to share with my subscribers. Throughout middle school and especially high school, I found that my confidence grew with my channel. And that's one reason (among many!) why I love my subscribers so much. They may not have known it at the time, but every comment of "This cake was a huge hit with my family!" and "Always look forward to your videos!" bolstered my self-esteem. I hope to repay them as best as I can by bringing a little sweetness into their life as well with recipes and tutorials for tasty, fun, and, best of all, *kawaii* sweet treats!

It has always been a dream of mine to write a book—one that focuses equally on baking *and* decorating delicious treats. I've cherished this opportunity to make my dream a reality! As I wrote, my hopes were twofold. One, I wanted all of the recipes here to be absolutely delicious. Not a single one of them is a throw-away, just a vehicle for cuteness. I worked hard on the base recipes so that you will not only love the kawaii decorations, but you'll also *crave* these sweets and be excited to make them anytime, whether you plan to decorate them or not. Second, I didn't want anyone to feel like the techniques were out of reach. Both novice and expert cake decorators will find these projects attainable, as I've used accessible tools and candies and have provided step-by-step instructions, many times accompanied with a photograph. Finally, I dearly hope that the fun photography and sweetly designed pages make you smile when you flip through this color-packed book and that it becomes a go-to source of dessert inspiration. I hope that this book makes you so excited to bake that it becomes full of notes written in the margins, dog-eared pages, and the occasional chocolate stain here and there.

So preheat your oven and break out the measuring cups—let's get started!

MUCH LOVE AND HUGS!

RACHEL

WHAT IS KAWAII?

Before we start baking, let's talk about what *kawaii* means! *Kawaii* is a Japanese word that best translates to "cute," and it describes anything lovable, cuddly, and endearing. The particular style of it is like Hello Kitty, Pokémon, and Totoro. It often manifests in cute animals (both real and illustrated) with big eyes and heads that are disproportionately large in relation to their bodies. These features emphasize an innocence and youthfulness that is a major component of kawaii style. And beyond cute cuddly creatures, kawaii also frequently means adding a face to something that normally wouldn't have one. For example, see the smiling Sushi Cake Pops on page 197 or the Kawaii Royal Icing Cookies on page 106. These lovable expressions add personality to the otherwise inanimate objects, making them extra-cute or "kawaii."

Kawaii culture is believed to have originated in the 1970s when teenagers in Japan developed a fun, childlike style of handwriting that was often accompanied by doodles of hearts, stars, and cartoon faces. Many believe this trend emerged in response to the rigidity of post–World War II Japan, as it allowed the Japanese youth to express their individuality. The Japanese stationery brand Sanrio noticed this movement and subsequently launched their cultural icon, Hello Kitty. A huge success among the Japanese population, Hello Kitty took the world by storm, ushering in a worldwide appreciation of kawaii. These days, kawaii style is used for all kinds of clothing, accessories, plush, stationery, and more! It has truly become a global cultural phenomenon, and one that I adore because of how fun, colorful, and inviting it is.

HOW TO USE THIS BOOK

This book is divided into seven chapters chock-full of tasty kawaii recipes. First up is the cakes chapter! I've always loved 6-inch layer cakes because I think they're the perfect size, so this chapter features many creations baked in this diameter. For instance, check out the adorable chocolate Panda Cake (page 54) or the Bunny Carrot Cake, complete with chocolate ears (page 59). The slightly-smaller-than-standard size makes them extra-kawaii, but still plenty substantial for any occasion.

Then it's on to some cute cupcake recipes. Cupcakes are perfect for parties because each person gets his or her own mini cake, and you have dozens of opportunities to make each treat unique. I'll show you how to transform ordinary (but tasty!) vanilla cupcakes into whimsical Unicorn Cupcakes (page 73) and my favorite chocolate cupcakes into charming Raccoon Cupcakes (page 67) with the help of some chocolate details. And even if you don't have time to decorate two dozen treats, you can always decorate a handful and add rainbow sprinkles to the rest! I love how sprinkles make any treat instantly kawaii.

Next up, we have the cookies chapter. Cookies transport easily, making them ideal for packing into lunch boxes or placing into cellphone bags for gifts. Some of my favorite ones for gifting are the Kawaii Royal Icing Cookies (page 106) and the Cupcake Piñata Cookies (page 93) because they're so colorful and you can easily customize them with different colors of icing and types of designs.

After that comes the pies and pastries chapter. In this one, I've provided recipes for both standard 8- or 9-inch pies and some fun pastries like Pig Cream Puffs (page 131) and Rainbow Fruit Tarts (page 144).

Next, it's on to bars and brownies. This chapter features recipes for both brownies and other treats that are baked in a "brownie pan" and cut into shapes. There are rich, fudgy Zebra Cheesecake-Brownie Bars (page 172), with beautiful swirls of brownie and cheesecake, and light, crumbly Lemon Bars (page 158).

Next, it's time for cake pops. If you've never had one, cake pops are essentially balls made out of cake and frosting mixed together that are then given a candy coating, and often they're decorated. They're not only delicious but also perfect for kawaii decoration because they can take on all different shapes and colors.

And finally, we have the chapter on candies and other sweets! Here you'll find candies like Chocolate Turtle Turtles (page 213) and Kawaii-Style Chocolate Truffles (page 217), as well as sweets like Mermaid Mint Ice Cream (page 214) and Coffee Flavored Doughnut Marshmallows (page 225). All in all, there's a dessert for everyone, so have fun flipping through this book and taking your pick!

For each recipe, there are instructions for both how to bake and how to decorate the dessert. When I created these recipes, I kept in mind that these two aspects are equally important. Not only did I want the desserts to look amazing, but I took special care to make sure they taste just as good as they look. For instance, I made eleven different versions of the chocolate cake recipe to get it *just* right! So rest assured that these recipes are not just a canvas for the painting. Rather, they're developed with flavor, texture, *and* appearance in mind.

Some of these desserts also require templates, which you can find in the back of this book. For instance, since it can be tricky to draw bunny ears freehand with melted chocolate, I've provided a template for the Bunny Carrot Cake ears (see page 230). To use a template, simply trace it onto a piece of parchment paper using a pencil, then flip the parchment paper over. You'll be able to see the shape through the paper while you work with the edible ingredients on the other side (be careful not to use the side with the pencil markings—you don't want pencil lead in your treats!).

INGREDIENTS

For the most part, baking ingredients are simple and straightforward. There are a handful, though, that I find give your sweets an extra-delicious edge. Here's what you need to stock in your pantry so every baking endeavor will be a success!

CAKE FLOUR: This type of flour, which you can find at most grocery stores, produces a more tender crumb than regular all-purpose flour. I find that the difference between the two isn't noticeable in every recipe, but for vanilla cake, cake flour does make a significant difference. Keep a bag on hand to make the most tender, moist, and delicious birthday cakes you can imagine!

INSTANT ESPRESSO POWDER: This handy ingredient helps make chocolate taste richer—I kid you not! You won't taste the coffee flavor; it'll just enhance the flavor of your chocolate ingredients, such as cocoa powder or melted semisweet chocolate. I've listed espresso powder as optional in this book (for example, in the Penguin Brownies recipe on page 151), but even though the recipes are great without it, I highly recommend adding it for that extra punch of flavor.

CHOCOLATE CHIPS: Whether you're using them in the recipe itself or using them for decoration, I recommend that you buy good-quality chips for extra yum! You should love the flavor of the chocolate chips on their own—nothing too sweet or too bitter. My favorite brands are Callebaut, Ghirardelli, and Trader Joe's.

COCOA POWDER: The recipes in this book use natural unsweetened cocoa powder, not Dutch-process cocoa powder. Natural unsweetened cocoa powder is less expensive and more widely available than Dutch-process, and it won't interfere with the leavening of your desserts the way Dutch-process can.

CANDY COATING: Candy coating is essentially a type of chocolate that doesn't require tempering in order for it to set properly. This makes it perfect for dipping cake pops and making chocolate decorations. It comes in two main varieties: Candiquik and candy melts.

CANDIQUIK: Bars of candy coating that come in microwave-safe trays, Candiquik melts down much smoother than candy melts do straight out of the package. The downside is that it only comes in white and chocolate, but you can color it yourself using oil-based food color. (Note that oil-based food color is *not* the same thing as liquid or gel. A set of oil-based food colors can be purchased online or at a craft store.) I think the added coloring step is well worth it. I've spent lots of time dealing with burnt thick candy melts, and Candiquik takes out all of the guesswork of thinning candy coating. Candiquik can be found in the baking aisle at most major grocery stores.

CANDY MELTS: These precolored wafers are made of compound chocolate and can be purchased at craft stores. They come in a rainbow of colors. The coating is quite thick once melted, so if you plan to use candy melts, you will need to thin them out with coconut oil or paramount crystals (which can be purchased online). Start by adding ½ teaspoon coconut oil or paramount crystals for every 8 ounces of candy melts, and then continue adding more coconut oil or paramount crystals, ½ teaspoon at a time, until the candy coating has the consistency of liquid glue. Because candy melts require this thinner and burn easily in the microwave, I prefer to use Candiquik to dip my cake pops. But I use the unmelted wafers as decorations all the time! Their round shape is perfect for eyes, ears, and many other details.

DECORATING ICING: Premade icing, sold in a plastic tube, is great to have on hand for piping on kawaii faces. It's available at most grocery stores, and you can even attach a piping tip directly onto the end of the tube with the help of a coupler (which can be found at a craft store). I recommend picking up a Wilton brand tube each of black, white, and pink icings to get started. And since kawaii faces are so small, it'll last you a long time! Well worth the buy.

UNSALTED BUTTER: Technically, you should always use unsalted butter for baking so you can control the salt content of your final baked good. Here's the thing, though: I've used both interchangeably for years, and have never noticed either blandness or saltiness. Standard grocery store butter just doesn't have *that much* salt in it, and the difference is usually negligible. So if you use salted butter instead, I'll look the other way!

SUBSTITUTIONS

Substitutions are often necessary when it comes to baking. I know from experience! I frequently go to the store to buy flour, buttermilk, and eggs and then come home with a new dress, a cute mug, and a throw blanket. Whoops! So I've become adept at making the following substitutions:

BUTTERMILK: Pour 1 tablespoon of white vinegar into a glass measuring cup, then fill the cup up to the 1-cup measure with milk. Stir, then let it sit at room temperature for at least 5 minutes before using.

SOUR CREAM: Use an equal amount of buttermilk or of full-fat Greek or regular yogurt for sour cream. And yes, you can use the buttermilk substitute, above, as a substitute for sour cream. Sneaky but effective!

CAKE FLOUR: Measure 1 cup of flour, put it into a bowl, and remove 2 tablespoons. Whisk in 2 tablespoons of cornstarch. While this substitution will work in a pinch, I highly recommend using the real-deal cake flour when you remember to buy it. It's worth it and does produce a noticeable difference from the substitute!

THE BEST CANDIES

These are the candies I use most frequently. Over the years, I've curated quite the collection of smoothers, gummy candies, chocolates, and more that I find helpful for creating kawaii treats. After all, the more candies used, the easier decorating is because there's less freehand piping required!

A M&M's
B Confetti quins
C Rainbow jimmies
D Rainbow sour strips
E Candy melts
F Rainbow nonpareils
G Giant heart sprinkles
H Rainbow sprinkle mix 1
I Confetti sprinkles
J Gummy fish
K Star sprinkles
L Mini M&M's
M Giant flower sprinkles
N Peanut M&M's
O Starburst
P Rainbow sprinkle mix 2
Q Jelly beans
R Mini marshmallows
S Flower sprinkles

THE BEST TOOLS

Some of these, like spatulas and measuring cups, are essential to any kind of baking endeavor, and some, like piping bags and icing smoothers, are specific to the decorating process. All of the decorating supplies can easily be found in the baking aisle of any craft store (including the special equipment necessary for the recipes in the Cake Pops and Candy & Other Sweets chapters).

A Piping bags
B Whisk
C Cookie dough scoop
D Offset spatula
E Wooden spoon
F Edible ink marker
G Tweezers
H Silicone bowls
I Icing smoother
J Measuring cups
K Measuring spoons
L Piping tips
M Rolling pin with thickness guides
N Toothpicks
O Rubber spatula

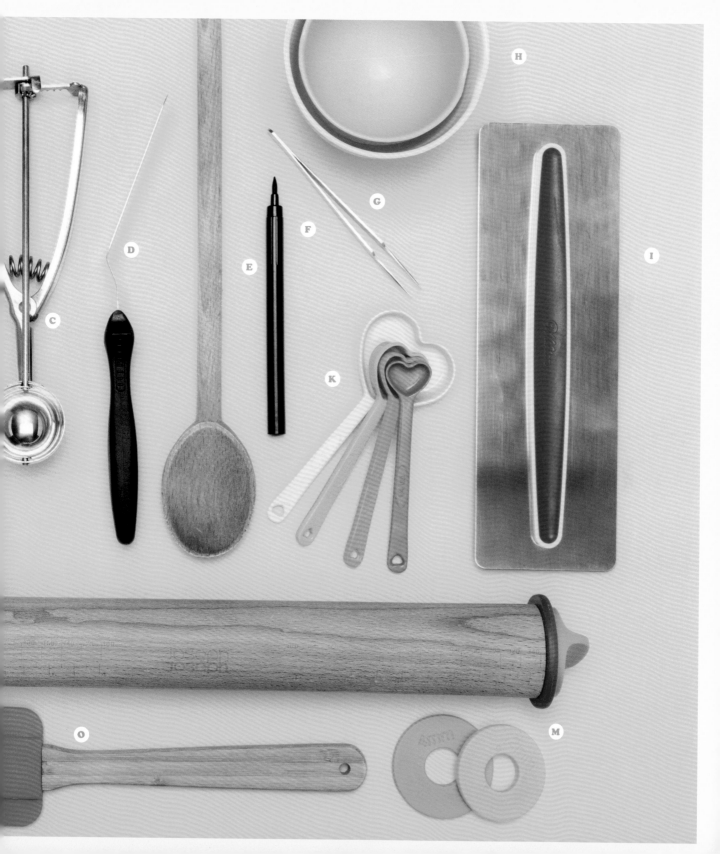

TOOLS

While specialized cake-decorating tools are not necessary to make cute treats, a few staples will certainly go a long way. Here are my top picks:

OFFSET SPATULA: This guy is a must for smoothing frostings, batters, or anything spreadable for that matter. The angle of the spatula makes decorating cakes a pinch! You can always use a rubber spatula or a butter knife if you don't have an offset spatula, but for a few bucks it'll make your life easier and smoother. I recommend picking up a small, 4½-inch one for use on cakes, cupcakes, and lots more.

ICING SMOOTHER: Icing smoothers have a big, flat edge that allows you to smooth the entire side of a cake at once (see pages 20–21). To use one, simply align the icing smoother with the side of the cake at a 30-degree angle. While you hold the smoother steady in one hand, use your other hand to turn the cake plate or turntable. You may have to stop two or three times to scrape excess frosting from the smoother. The end result will be a smooth, straight edge along the side of your cake.

CAKE TURNTABLE: If you plan to make lots of kawaii cakes, one of these is a huge help. It'll allow you to work around the sides of the cake quickly, and smoothing icing along the sides of the cake will be much easier as well.

PIPING TIPS: Piping tips provide you with more precision than simply snipping the tip off a piping bag or a plastic zip-top bag. I find that snipping off a tip gives you an oval shape rather than a perfect circle, with the result that your piping may not come out exactly as you hope. When piping small details like kawaii faces, piping tips are especially handy. The one time I avoid them is when I'm going to pipe chocolate because no one wants to clean hardened chocolate out of a tiny piping tip!

PIPING BAGS: I like to buy piping bags in bulk online. I'll reach for a piping bag over a plastic zip-top bag if I plan to use a piping tip or if I want to fill it with more than 2 cups of frosting or batter. This is because gallon-size plastic zip-top bags can be a bit awkward to handle for neat piping.

MEASURING CUPS + SPOONS: Life hack: buy a set of measuring spoons that has the "unconventional" measurements. Look for the ⅛ teaspoon and the ½ tablespoon (which is the same as 1½ teaspoons). It'll make halving recipes super-simple. No more guesstimating those little measurements!

RUBBER SPATULA: I prefer the thin, flexible kind because they really help you scrape every last bit of frosting or cake batter from the bowl. It's a great triple-duty tool for mixing, folding, and scraping.

TWEEZERS: I love using tweezers to place decorations and sprinkles on top of cakes and cupcakes. Not only do they provide excellent precision, but they also make me feel like some sort of cake surgeon. Fun!

BAKING TECHNIQUES AND TRICKS

If you follow the instructions for the recipes in this book, I feel confident that you'll turn out some very tasty treats. However, there are several extra steps that are worth taking to reach the full potential of each sweet. So take note of these tips and you'll be baking like a pro!

ROOM-TEMPERATURE INGREDIENTS: Before you get started baking, make sure to bring all of your ingredients to room temperature. This is especially important for eggs, butter, and milk. Otherwise, your ingredients won't incorporate as smoothly when you mix them. You'll end up with a lumpy batter and it'll make you sad. Let's avoid that. (See sidebar at right for some help.)

MELTING CHOCOLATE: Throughout this book you'll notice that melted chocolate is often called for to pipe on kawaii faces and other fun details. To melt chocolate in the microwave, place the chocolate chips in a microwave-safe bowl and microwave at 20-second intervals, stirring in between each interval, until smooth. To melt chocolate over the stove, I recommend filling a small saucepan with 3 inches of water and then bringing it to a boil. Turn the heat down to medium and place a heatproof bowl on top and add the chocolate to the bowl. Stir the chocolate until it's fully melted.

CREAMING BUTTER + SUGAR: Beating butter and sugar together takes longer than you may expect! In a stand mixer or using an electric hand mixer, make sure to cream the butter and sugar together for at least 3 to 4 minutes. The mixture should be fluffy and lightened in color to a pale yellow. You can also cream butter and sugar together by hand, although it will require some elbow grease: Combine the butter and sugar using a wooden spoon, then use a fork to whip the mixture until no more streaks of butter remain and the mixture is light and fluffy. Properly creamed butter and sugar results in light cakes and

ROOM-TEMPERATURE SHORTCUTS

I know I said to let these ingredients come to room temperature before you bake, but let's be real. When you want cookies, you want them now! Here are my tips on getting ingredients to room temperature fast.

BUTTER + CREAM CHEESE: Cut the butter or cream cheese into about 1-inch cubes, and place the cubes in a microwave-safe dish. Microwave the cubes on one side for 5 to 10 seconds (depending on the strength of your microwave), then flip them onto another side and microwave for 5 to 10 more seconds. The butter or cream cheese should be soft but not melted.

EGGS: Place the uncracked eggs in a bowl of warm (not hot) water and let them sit for at least 10 minutes.

MILK + SOUR CREAM: Pour the milk or sour cream into a microwave-safe jug or glass and microwave for 15 seconds. Stir to evenly distribute the heat, then microwave for additional 15-second intervals, stirring after each interval, as necessary to bring the milk or sour cream to room temperature. For the recipes in this book, I recommend at least 2% milk for optimal flavor.

chewy cookies. Don't skimp on the process and you'll reap the benefits!

REVERSE CREAMING METHOD FOR VANILLA CAKE: I kid you not when I say I have made at least a *dozen* variations of vanilla cake to find my absolute favorite dream recipe. The "reverse creaming" method is a little unconventional, but it's totally easy. The technique allows the butter to coat every particle of flour, which prevents the formation of gluten (which is what makes cakes tougher and "chewier" in a bad way). Mixing the fat into the flour also results in smaller air pockets and a finer, more tender crumb. Yay science!

Here's how you do it: In a stand mixer fitted with the paddle attachment, you mix together the dry ingredients until combined. Then you add cubed room-temperature butter right into the dry ingre-dients and mix on medium-low speed until the mixture resembles fine sand. While that mixes, whisk together your wet ingredients in a bowl. Then just pour the wet ingredients into the dry and mix until combined! It's easy as that, and it produces a cake that's moist and tender, but still dense enough to hold up to frostings for layer cakes. The key is that all your ingredients must be at room temperature, and in fact I like the milk to be a little warm. When it comes to the butter, I recommend you cube it while cold and then let the butter come to room temperature, because soft butter is a bit tricky to cut evenly. Otherwise, if you work with cold ingredients, you'll get a lumpy batter that'll still produce a tasty cake, albeit with a bumpier texture. I'm absolutely *in love* with the technique, and I know you'll love it, too!

I frequently reference small, medium, and large round piping tips throughout the book. This translates to:

Small: Wilton size 1, 2, or 3 (about ¹⁄₁₆-inch diameter)
Medium: Wilton size 11 or 12 (about ¼-inch diameter)
Large: Wilton size 1A (about ½-inch diameter)

STORING BAKED GOODS

In general, baked goods should be stored in airtight containers and kept for 3 to 5 days while they still retain their texture, moisture content, and freshness. Desserts that should be refrigerated are denoted throughout this book.

This vanilla cake recipe takes really well to different flavorings. Here are some of my favorites:

CINNAMON-SPICE
Add 1 tablespoon of cinnamon to the dry ingredients.

LEMON
Add 2 tablespoons of grated lemon zest to the wet ingredients.

BERRY
Toss 1½ cups of your favorite berries with 1 tablespoon of flour, and then fold them into the prepared batter.

CORGI CAKE

MAKES
ONE 6-INCH
LAYER CAKE

If you want a cake that will make someone smile the instant they see it, *this is the cake.* There's something about its small, sweet smile and cute, perky ears that melts hearts. And the best part? It's simple, too! Thanks to using toasted coconut for the fur, there's no need for a fancy decorating technique to achieve a corgi's signature fluff.

FOR THE CAKE

Cooking spray

3 cups cake flour

2 cups sugar

2 teaspoons baking powder

½ teaspoon baking soda

1 teaspoon table salt

½ cup (1 stick) unsalted butter,
    cut into ½-inch cubes, at room
    temperature

4 eggs, at room temperature

1 cup buttermilk, at room temperature

½ cup canola oil

4 teaspoons vanilla extract

FOR THE FROSTING

1½ cups (3 sticks) unsalted butter,
    at room temperature

4½ cups confectioners' sugar

1½ teaspoons vanilla extract

3 tablespoons milk

Black gel food color

1. MAKE THE CAKE: Preheat the oven to 350°F. Spray three 6-inch round cake pans with cooking spray. Line the pans with parchment paper and lightly spray again.

2. In a stand mixer fitted with the paddle attachment, combine the cake flour, sugar, baking powder, baking soda, and salt on low speed until well mixed, about 1 minute. With the mixer running on low speed, add the cubed butter and beat until the mixture resembles coarse sand, about 4 minutes. (For more on this technique, see page 23.)

3. In a separate bowl, whisk together the eggs, buttermilk, oil, and vanilla. With the mixer running on low speed, gradually add the wet ingredients to the dry ingredients, and beat just until combined. Divide the batter evenly among the prepared pans.

4. Bake until a toothpick inserted into the centers of the cakes comes out clean, 35 to 40 minutes. Let the cakes cool in the pans for 10 minutes. Then run a knife around the edges of the pans and turn the cakes out onto a cooling rack. Peel off the parchment paper and let them cool completely.

5. MAKE THE FROSTING: In a stand mixer fitted with the paddle

attachment, beat the butter on high speed until smooth, about 1 minute. Reduce the speed to low, gradually add the confectioners' sugar, and beat until combined. Beat in the vanilla and milk until combined. Scrape down the sides of the bowl. Beat the frosting on medium-high speed until it is light and fluffy, about 3 minutes.

6. Transfer 1 tablespoon of the frosting to a separate bowl and dye it black with black gel food color. Transfer the black frosting to a small plastic zip-top bag and cut off a small tip.

7. Transfer 1 tablespoon of the remaining white frosting to a small plastic zip-top bag and cut off a small tip.

8. Transfer the remaining frosting to a piping bag or to a large plastic zip-top bag and cut off a large tip.

9. DECORATE THE CAKE: Preheat the oven to 325°F. Line a small baking sheet with parchment paper.

10. Spread the coconut evenly on the prepared baking sheet. Toast it until it is golden brown, 5 to 10 minutes, stirring it with a spatula every 3 minutes for even browning. Keep a close eye on it to make sure it does not burn. Let the coconut cool completely.

(recipe and ingredients continue)

2 cups sweetened flaked coconut

1 graham cracker

1 chocolate chip

2 chocolate-covered espresso beans

2 pink jelly beans

11. Using a serrated knife, cut the graham cracker in half widthwise. Cut off the two upper corners on each piece to form a point. Pipe white frosting over the front side of the graham crackers and spread it evenly with an offset spatula to cover the cracker. Press coconut onto the frosting. Repeat on the back sides of the crackers. Set the corgi ears and the remaining coconut aside.

12. Using a cake leveler or a serrated knife, cut the rounded tops off the cakes. Pipe about 1 tablespoon of white frosting from the large piping bag onto a 6-inch cake board, and then place one cake layer on top. Pipe a layer of white frosting onto the cake and spread it evenly with an offset spatula. Place another cake layer on top, pipe on a layer of white frosting, and spread the frosting evenly with an offset spatula. Top with the final cake layer, placing the cut side down. For the crumb coat, pipe a thin layer of white frosting over the entire cake and spread it evenly with an offset spatula. Refrigerate the cake for 15 minutes.

13. Pipe white frosting over the entire cake and spread it evenly with an offset spatula. Run an icing smoother over the sides of the cake to smooth the frosting. Using an offset spatula, bring the frosting from the top edges of the cake toward the center to create a flat top. Refrigerate the cake until the frosting is firm to the touch and doesn't stick to your finger, about 20 minutes.

14. Using the template (see page 232), trace the corgi face and head onto a sheet of parchment paper, and then cut them out. Gently press the cut-out corgi face template against the front of the chilled cake. Then press the cut-out corgi head template on the top of the cake, making sure to line it up with the face template. Apply only enough pressure to adhere the template—you don't want to leave fingerprints in the frosting!

15. Grab handfuls of the coconut and press them against the cake. Refrigerate the cake until the frosting is firm again, about 15 minutes. Then carefully peel away the templates.

16. Press the side of the chocolate chip into the front of the cake for a nose, and then pipe on a mouth beneath the nose with the black frosting.

17. Press the two chocolate-covered espresso beans into the cake for eyes, and then pipe on the eyebrows with the small bag of white frosting. Press the pink jelly beans on the sides of the cake for cheeks, beside the eyes.

18. Use a knife to make two slits in the top of the cake as a guide for the ear placement, and then place one ear in each slit.

CAT CAKE

MAKES
ONE 7-INCH
CAKE

Little-known fact: Growing up, I was absolutely terrified of animals. One of my most poignant memories related to this detail of my life is the time my mom and I (about seven years old) went to a neighbor's house, and their cute, friendly calico cat decided to come say hello and lick my hand. And you know what I did? *I started crying.* My poor, embarrassed mom stammered out, "Oh, she's fine! No, she's not allergic—uh, we should probably get going. . . ." Thankfully, I've since gotten over this fear and have commemorated that sweet cat with this cake. I promise it won't bite!

FOR THE CAKE
Cooking spray

2¼ cups cake flour

1½ cups sugar

1½ teaspoons baking powder

¼ teaspoon baking soda

¾ teaspoon table salt

6 tablespoons unsalted butter, cut into ½-inch cubes, at room temperature

3 large eggs, at room temperature

¾ cup buttermilk, at room temperature

6 tablespoons canola oil

1 tablespoon vanilla extract

FOR THE FROSTING
1½ cups (3 sticks) unsalted butter, at room temperature

4½ cups confectioners' sugar

1½ teaspoons vanilla extract

3 tablespoons milk

Black and orange gel food color

1. MAKE THE CAKE: Preheat the oven to 325°F. Generously spray a 1.5-quart ovenproof bowl with cooking spray and line a baking sheet with foil.

2. In a stand mixer fitted with the paddle attachment, combine the cake flour, sugar, baking powder, baking soda, and salt on low speed until well mixed, about 1 minute. With the mixer on low speed, add the cubed butter and mix until the mixture resembles coarse sand, about 4 minutes. (For more on this technique, see page 23.)

3. In a separate medium bowl, whisk together the eggs, buttermilk, oil, and vanilla. With the mixer on low speed, gradually add the wet ingredients to the dry ingredients and beat just until combined. Pour the batter into the prepared bowl, and put the bowl on top of the prepared baking sheet (in case any batter overflows during baking).

4. Bake until a skewer inserted into the center of the cake comes out clean, 80 to 85 minutes.

5. Let the cake cool in the bowl for 10 minutes. Using a serrated knife, level off the top of cake. Then run a knife around the sides of the bowl, being careful not to cut into the cake Flip the cake out onto a wire rack and let it cool completely.

6. MAKE THE FROSTING: In a stand mixer fitted with the paddle attachment, beat the butter on high speed until smooth, about 1 minute. Reduce the speed to low and gradually add the confectioners' sugar and beat until combined. Add the vanilla and milk and beat until combined. Scrape down the sides of the bowl. Beat the frosting on medium-high speed until it is light and fluffy, about 3 minutes.

7. Transfer ¼ cup plus 1 tablespoon of the frosting to a separate bowl and color it black with the black gel food color. Transfer 1 tablespoon of the black frosting to a small plastic zip-top bag and cut off a small tip. Transfer the remaining black frosting to a piping bag fitted with a star tip.

(recipe and ingredients continue)

CAKES

FOR THE DECORATIONS

1 graham cracker

2 chocolate candy melts

1 chocolate chip

2 pink jelly beans

8. Transfer ¼ cup of the remaining white frosting to a separate bowl and color it orange with the orange gel food color. Transfer the orange frosting to a piping bag fitted with a star tip. Transfer the remaining white frosting to a piping bag fitted with a star tip.

9. **DECORATE THE CAKE:** Using a serrated knife, cut the graham cracker in half widthwise. Cut off the two upper corners on each piece to form a point. To place the ears, cut a slit on each side of the cake at least as wide as the graham cracker, then nestle the ears in the slits.

10. Pipe stars all over the left ear with the large piping bag of black frosting. Repeat with the orange frosting for the right ear. Then pipe white stars over the rest of the cake.

11. Pipe a small amount of white frosting onto each chocolate candy melt for a pupil and smooth it with a toothpick. Press the side of a chocolate chip into the front of the cake for a nose, and then place the candy melt eyes on both sides.

12. Press a pink jelly bean on each side of the cake, beside the eyes. Pipe a smile beneath the nose with the small bag of black frosting.

I could eat sushi every day for the rest of my life and be perfectly content. I love it all! From simple yellowtail sashimi to those over-the-top works of art composed of tempura shrimp and multiple special sauces, sushi is truly the way to my heart. The candies on this cake represent some of my favorite fillings: salmon sashimi, tamago, avocado, and roe. Make this cake and you can have sushi for dinner *and* dessert!

FOR THE CAKE

Cooking spray

1½ cups all-purpose flour

1½ cups sugar

⅔ cup natural unsweetened cocoa powder

1½ teaspoons baking soda

¾ teaspoon baking powder

1 teaspoon table salt

2 large eggs, at room temperature

¾ cup buttermilk, at room temperature

6 tablespoons canola oil

1 teaspoon vanilla extract

¾ cup hot coffee

FOR THE CHOCOLATE FROSTING

1½ cups (3 sticks) unsalted butter, at room temperature

4 cups confectioners' sugar

¾ cup natural unsweetened cocoa powder

⅓ cup milk

1 teaspoon vanilla extract

1 teaspoon instant espresso powder (optional)

Black gel food color

FOR THE DECORATIONS

2 white candy melts

1 cup vanilla-flavored marshmallow bits (or mini marshmallows cut in half)

3 pink fruit-flavored candy chews, such as Starburst

1 red fruit-flavored candy chew, such as Starburst

3 tablespoons orange jelly beans

5 green fish-shaped gummy candies, cut into ¼-inch pieces

5 yellow fish-shaped gummy candies, cut into ¼-inch pieces

White decorating icing, fitted with a small round tip (I like Wilton brand)

2 pink jelly beans

---

1. **MAKE THE CAKE:** Preheat the oven to 350°F. Spray three 6-inch round cake pans with cooking spray. Line the pans with parchment paper and lightly spray again.

2. In a large bowl, whisk together the flour, sugar, cocoa powder, baking soda, baking powder, and salt. Add the eggs, buttermilk, oil, and vanilla, and using a handheld electric mixer, beat on medium speed until combined. Pour in the hot coffee and beat on medium speed until just combined. Divide the batter among the prepared pans.

3. Bake until a toothpick inserted into the centers of the cakes comes out clean, 27 to 30 minutes. Let the cakes cool in the pans for 10 minutes. Then run a knife around the edges and turn the cakes out onto a cooling rack. Peel off the parchment paper and let them cool completely.

4. **MAKE THE FROSTING:** In a stand mixer fitted with the paddle attachment, beat the butter on high speed until smooth, about 1 minute. Reduce the speed to low, gradually add the confectioners' sugar and cocoa powder, and beat until combined. Add the milk, vanilla extract, and espresso powder, if using, and beat on low speed until combined. Scrape down the sides of the bowl. Beat the frosting on medium-high speed until it is smooth and fluffy, about 2 minutes. Add in enough gel food color to achieve a deep black and beat until combined. Place the frosting in a piping bag or in a large plastic zip-top bag and cut off a small tip.

5. **DECORATE THE CAKE:** Pipe black frosting on the upper corner of the white candy melts for pupils, and set the eyes aside. Then cut off a larger tip on the piping bag.

6. Using a cake leveler or a serrated knife, cut the rounded tops off the cakes. Pipe about 1 tablespoon of the black frosting onto a 6-inch cake board, then place one cake layer on top. Pipe a layer of black frosting onto the cake and spread it evenly with an offset spatula. Place another cake layer on top, pipe on a layer of black frosting, and spread the frosting evenly with an offset spatula. Top with the final cake layer, placing the cut side down. For the crumb coat, pipe a thin layer of black frosting over the entire cake and spread it evenly with an offset spatula. Refrigerate the cake for 15 minutes.

7. Pipe black frosting over the entire cake and spread it evenly with an offset spatula. Run an icing smoother over the sides of the cake to smooth the frosting. Using an offset spatula, bring the frosting from the top edges of the cake toward the center to create a flat top.

8. Press the marshmallow bits on top of the cake for the "rice," leaving a ¾-inch border around the edge.

9. Microwave the pink and red fruit-flavored candy chews for 5 seconds to soften them. Then mold the pink chews together to form a half-moon for the "sashimi." Roll the red chew into a thin snake, then lightly press diagonal stripes of the red on top of the pink. Lay the "sashimi" on top of the "rice."

10. Place the orange jelly beans opposite the sashimi for the "roe."

11. Place the gummy fish pieces near the roe for the tamago and avocado.

12. Pipe a smile onto the cake using the white decorating icing, and then press the eyes beside the smile. Press the pink jelly bean cheeks onto the cake beside the eyes.

RAMEN BOWL CAKE

Have you ever eaten a food so frequently that you had to take an extended break from it? That happened to me with ramen. The chewy noodles, the rich broth, and all the different toppings—bamboo shoots, hard-boiled egg, fish cakes, scallions—are totally addictive. While I managed to refrain from eating the dish all the time, I couldn't get it off my mind. So I turned it into cake! This is one of my "gravity-defying" cakes—a fun technique of suspending something in the air over the cake. Though it looks kind of fancy and makes a big impression, it's very simple to put together.

FOR THE CAKE

Cooking spray

2¼ cups cake flour

1½ cups sugar

1½ teaspoons baking powder

¼ teaspoon baking soda

¾ teaspoon table salt

6 tablespoons unsalted butter, cut into ½-inch cubes, at room temperature

3 large eggs, at room temperature

¾ cup buttermilk, at room temperature

6 tablespoons canola oil

1 tablespoon vanilla extract

FOR THE FROSTING

1½ cups (3 sticks) unsalted butter, at room temperature

4½ cups confectioners' sugar

1½ teaspoons vanilla extract

3 tablespoons milk

Yellow and black gel food color

1. **MAKE THE CAKE:** Preheat the oven to 325°F. Spray a 1.5-quart ovenproof bowl generously with cooking spray and line a baking sheet with foil.

2. In a stand mixer fitted with the paddle attachment, combine the cake flour, sugar, baking powder, baking soda, and salt on low speed until well mixed, about 1 minute. With the mixer running on low speed, add the cubed butter and beat until the mixture resembles coarse sand, about 4 minutes. (For more on this technique, see page 23.)

3. In a separate medium bowl, whisk together the eggs, buttermilk, oil, and vanilla. With the mixer running on low speed, gradually add the wet ingredients to the dry ingredients and beat just until combined. Pour the batter into the prepared bowl, and then place the bowl on the prepared baking sheet (in case any batter overflows during baking).

4. Bake until a skewer inserted into the center of the cake comes out clean, 80 to 85 minutes. Let the cake cool for 10 minutes in the bowl. Using a serrated knife, level off the top of the cake. Then run a knife around the edges of the bowl, being careful not to cut into the cake. Flip the cake out onto a wire rack and let it cool completely.

5. **MAKE THE FROSTING:** In a stand mixer fitted with the paddle attachment, beat the butter on high speed until smooth, about 1 minute. Reduce the speed to low, gradually add the confectioners' sugar, and beat until combined. Beat in the vanilla and milk until combined. Scrape down the sides of the bowl. Beat the frosting on medium-high speed until it is light and fluffy, about 3 minutes. Transfer 1½ cups of the frosting to a separate bowl and color it pale yellow with yellow gel food color. Transfer the frosting to a piping bag fitted with a small round tip or to a plastic zip-top bag and cut off a small tip.

6. Color the remaining frosting black with a generous amount of black gel food color. Transfer 1 tablespoon of the black frosting to a small piping bag or to a small plastic zip-top bag and cut off a small tip.

7. Transfer the remaining black frosting to a piping bag or to a large plastic zip-top bag and cut off a large tip.

(recipe and ingredients continue)

If you find the fruit-flavored candy chews or soft caramels stick to your hands too much, dust your hands and the work surface with a bit of confectioners' sugar.

FOR THE DECORATIONS

4 ounces white candy coating, melted (about ¼ cup melted coating)

1 pink fruit-flavored candy chew, such as Starburst

1 yellow fruit-flavored candy chew, such as Starburst

3 soft light-colored square caramels

2 chopsticks

5 rainbow sour strips, such as Airheads Xtremes, or 2 green fish-shaped gummy candies

8. DECORATE THE CAKE: Place the cake on an 8-inch cake board so the larger diameter is facedown. For the crumb coat, pipe the black frosting over the cake and spread it into a thin layer. Refrigerate for 10 minutes.

9. Pipe black frosting over the entire cake and spread it evenly with an offset spatula. Run the spatula along the sides of the cake while turning the cake stand or cake turntable (if using) to create an even finish. Place a 6-inch cake board on top of the cake and use it to flip the cake over (so the side with the larger diameter is now facing up). Remove the 8-inch cake board from the top of the cake. Pipe a ring of black frosting around the outside of the rim of the cake to create the lip of the bowl.

10. On a sheet of parchment paper, spoon out three ovals of the melted white candy coating that are about 2 inches long; these are the "eggs" and the "fish cake." Let them set completely at room temperature, about

10 minutes. Then gently remove them from the parchment paper.

11. Microwave the fruit-flavored candy chews for 5 seconds to soften them. Reserving a pea-size amount of the yellow chew, press a small portion of the yellow candy chew on top of the flat side of two of the eggs to create yolks. Roll out the pink candy chew to form a thin log, and then press a swirl of the log on the flat side of the remaining oval to make a fish cake.

12. Using the reserved piece of yellow candy chew, glue the chopsticks together so that they cross. Lay the chopsticks down on a sheet of parchment paper and spoon the remaining melted white candy coating over them to make a 7-inch stick that extends down from the chopsticks (see photo 1); this will be used to stick the chopsticks into the cake, so make this stick as thick as possible to ensure that it is sturdy. Let it set completely at room temperature, about 15 minutes.

13. Pipe noodles on top of the cake using the pale yellow frosting. For random curls, hold the piping bag at least 5 inches above the cake while piping continuously.

14. For the bamboo shoots, mold the caramels into three rectangles and drag a toothpick across the surface to texture it with wavy lines.

15. If you are using rainbow sour strips for the green onions, cut off the green portion of the sour strips with kitchen scissors. Cut each green portion into 1¼-inch sections, and then wrap the strip into a circle and press the ends together to seal. Repeat for each sour

strip. If you are using green fish-shaped candies, cut them into small pieces using kitchen scissors.

16. Gently remove the chopsticks and the white candy coating stick from the parchment paper. Cut a slit in the top of the cake that is the width of the chocolate stick and gently place it inside the cake (see photos 2 and 3). Pipe more noodles on the chopsticks and on the chocolate stick to cover the chocolate (see photo 4).

17. Arrange the toppings in the ramen bowl, and then pipe kawaii faces onto the eggs and the fish cake, using the reserved black frosting.

HAMBURGER CAKE

I love that desserts like this one are dubbed "gravity-defying" (my Ramen Bowl Cake, page 36, is one of these, too). It makes it sound like this cake is about to be loaded onto a space shuttle and fed to a group of hungry astronauts. When I was dreaming up the idea for a hamburger cake, I couldn't imagine it without ketchup pouring all over it. It just seemed so fun and dynamic! Thanks to a super-easy technique for suspending a ketchup cup in the air, my dream became reality.

MAKES ONE
6-INCH LAYER
CAKE

FOR THE CAKE

Cooking spray

3 cups cake flour

2 cups sugar

2 teaspoons baking powder

½ teaspoon baking soda

1 teaspoon table salt

½ cup (1 stick) unsalted butter,
cut into ½-inch cubes,
at room temperature

4 large eggs, at room
temperature

1 cup buttermilk, at room
temperature

½ cup canola oil

4 teaspoons vanilla extract

FOR THE FROSTING

¾ cup (1½ sticks) unsalted
butter, at room temperature

2¼ cups confectioners' sugar

1 teaspoon vanilla extract

1 tablespoon milk

Red gel food color

3 tablespoons natural
unsweetened cocoa powder

1. **MAKE THE CAKE:** Preheat the oven to 350°F. Spray three 6-inch round cake pans with cooking spray. Line the pans with parchment paper and lightly spray again.

2. In a stand mixer fitted with the paddle attachment, combine the cake flour, sugar, baking powder, baking soda, and salt on low speed until well mixed, about 1 minute. With the mixer running on low speed, add the cubed butter and beat until the mixture resembles coarse sand, about 4 minutes. (For more on this technique, see page 23.)

3. In a separate bowl, whisk together the eggs, buttermilk, oil, and vanilla. With the mixer running on low speed, gradually add the wet ingredients to the dry ingredients and beat just until combined. Divide the batter evenly among the prepared pans.

4. Bake until a toothpick inserted into the center of the cakes comes out clean, 35 to 40 minutes. Let the cakes cool in the pans for 10 minutes. Then run a knife around the edges and turn the cakes out onto a cooling rack. Peel off the parchment paper and let them cool completely. Using a serrated knife, cut the rounded tops off two of the cakes.

5. **MAKE THE FROSTING:** In a stand mixer fitted with the paddle attachment, beat the butter on high speed until smooth, about 1 minute. Reduce the speed to low, gradually add the confectioners' sugar, and beat until combined. Beat in the vanilla and milk until combined. Scrape down the sides of the bowl. Beat the frosting on medium-high speed until it is light and fluffy, about 3 minutes.

6. Transfer 1 tablespoon of the frosting to a small piping bag or to a small plastic zip-top bag and cut off a small tip.

7. Transfer half of the remaining frosting to a separate bowl and color it red with the red gel food color, aiming to match the color of the red candy coating. Transfer the red frosting to a plastic zip-top bag and cut off a medium tip.

8. Color the remaining frosting brown with the cocoa powder. Transfer it to a plastic zip-top bag and cut off a small tip.

9. **DECORATE THE CAKE:** Place the ketchup cup on its side on a piece of parchment paper, and then spoon the melted red candy coating inside the cup and spread it downward so a "stick" of candy extends from the cup. Make this stick as thick as possible to ensure that it is sturdy. Let it set completely at room temperature, about 15 minutes.

10. Microwave the yellow fruit-flavored chews for 5 seconds to soften them, and then press each chew out into a flat square to make the cheese.

11. Pipe a small amount of the chocolate frosting on the upper corner of the white candy melts to make the eyes. Then cut a larger tip off the bag.

12. Place the flaked coconut in a large plastic zip-top bag and add two drops of green gel food color. Shake the bag to evenly distribute the color, adding more food color, if desired, to make the lettuce.

(recipe and ingredients continue)

Paper ketchup cup or paper cupcake wrapper, about 2 inches tall

2 ounces red candy coating, melted (about 2 tablespoons melted coating)

4 yellow fruit-flavored candy chews, such as Starburst

2 white candy melts

½ cup sweetened flaked coconut

Green gel food color

2 pink jelly beans

½ teaspoon white sesame seeds

13. Place one leveled cake layer on a serving plate. Use an offset spatula to spread a thin layer of the chocolate frosting on top of the leveled cake layer. Scatter the coconut "lettuce" on top, spreading it just slightly over the edges. Pipe a layer of red frosting over the coconut to create a tomato slice, and then set the "cheese" so it overhangs the red frosting.

14. Place the second leveled cake layer on top and spread a thin layer of chocolate frosting over it for a crumb coat. Refrigerate for 15 minutes. Then spread a final layer of frosting over the cake layer. Using the end of the offset spatula, create peaks and swirl the frosting around the sides of the chocolate layer to mimic a patty texture.

15. Gently remove the ketchup cup, with its candy ketchup stick, from the parchment paper. Cut a slit in the top of the cake at the point where you want the ketchup drizzle to fall, making sure the slit is at least the width of the ketchup stick. Carefully insert the ketchup stick inside the cake.

16. Pipe the red frosting on top of the cake for ketchup drizzle. Using an offset spatula, carefully spread the ketchup drizzle frosting up the stick slightly to blend.

17. Pipe a smile onto the front of the cake with the white frosting, and attach the eyes to both sides with small dots of frosting.

18. Pipe small dots of frosting on the backs of the pink jelly beans and place them on the sides of the cake for cheeks, beside the eyes.

19. Sprinkle the sesame seeds on the remaining cake layer, and then lean it against the cake to be the top bun.

TURTLE CAKE

MAKES
ONE 7-INCH
CAKE

Baking a cake in an ovenproof bowl is one of my favorite techniques for creating a dome shape using kitchen equipment you already own. No need to spend hours carving cake to get a perfectly rounded dome! This turtle cake uses the handy bowl-baking method to create a shell of tender, moist vanilla cake.

FOR THE CAKE
Cooking spray

2¼ cups cake flour

1½ cups sugar

1½ teaspoons baking powder

¼ teaspoon baking soda

¾ teaspoon table salt

6 tablespoons unsalted butter, cut into ½-inch cubes, at room temperature

3 large eggs, at room temperature

¾ cup buttermilk, at room temperature

6 tablespoons canola oil

1 tablespoon vanilla extract

FOR THE FROSTING
1 cup (2 sticks) unsalted butter, at room temperature

3 cups confectioners' sugar

1 teaspoon vanilla extract

2 tablespoons milk

Green gel food color

1. MAKE THE CAKE: Preheat the oven to 325°F. Generously spray a 1.5-quart ovenproof bowl with cooking spray and line a baking sheet with foil.

2. In a stand mixer fitted with the paddle attachment, combine the cake flour, sugar, baking powder, baking soda, and salt on low speed until well mixed, about 1 minute. With the mixer running on low speed, add the cubed butter and beat until the mixture resembles coarse sand, about 4 minutes. (For more on this technique, see page 23.)

3. In a separate medium bowl, whisk together the eggs, buttermilk, oil, and vanilla. With the mixer running on low speed, gradually add the wet ingredients to the dry ingredients and beat just until combined. Pour the batter into the prepared bowl, and then place the bowl on top of the prepared baking sheet (in case any batter overflows during baking).

4. Bake until a skewer inserted into the center of the cake comes out clean, 80 to 85 minutes. Let the cake cool in the bowl for 10 minutes. Using a serrated knife, level off the top of cake. Then run a knife around the sides of the bowl, being careful not to cut into the cake. Flip the cake out onto a wire rack and let it cool completely.

5. MAKE THE FROSTING: In a stand mixer fitted with the paddle attachment, beat the butter on high speed until smooth, about 1 minute. Reduce the speed to low, gradually add the confectioners' sugar, and beat until combined. Beat in the vanilla and milk until combined. Scrape down the sides of the bowl. Beat the frosting on medium-high speed until it is light and fluffy, about 3 minutes.

6. Color all of the frosting green with the green gel food color. Transfer ¼ cup of the frosting to a separate bowl and add more green gel food color to dye it a darker green. Transfer the dark green frosting to a small piping bag fitted with a small round tip or to a small plastic zip-top bag and cut off a small tip. Transfer the remaining frosting to a piping bag or to a large plastic zip-top bag and cut off a large tip.

7. MAKE THE MARSHMALLOW TREATS: In a large microwave-safe bowl, microwave the marshmallows in 30-second intervals, stirring after each interval, until melted, about 3 minutes total. Color the melted marshmallows green with green gel food color. Using a rubber spatula, fold in the crisped rice cereal. Let the mixture sit until

(recipe and ingredients continue)

FOR THE MARSHMALLOW TREATS

2 cups mini marshmallows

Green gel food color

3 cups crisped rice cereal

FOR THE DECORATIONS

2 chocolate chips

¼ teaspoon melted white candy melts
(optional)

1 teaspoon melted chocolate chips

1 pink fruit-flavored candy chew,
such as Starburst

it is cool enough to handle, about
5 minutes.

8. Using slightly wet hands, mold about 1 cup of the marshmallow treats to form the turtle's head. Then mold about ½ cup of the treat mixture into a cylinder; repeat to make a second cylinder. Cut the cylinders in half crosswise on a diagonal; these are the arms and legs. Finally, mold ¼ cup of the treat mixture into a cone for the tail.

9. DECORATE THE CAKE: Pipe a small amount of the lighter green frosting on a cake board and transfer the cake to the board. For the crumb coat, pipe the lighter green frosting over the cake and use an offset spatula to spread it into a thin layer. Refrigerate the cake for 10 minutes.

10. Pipe more light green frosting over the entire cake and spread it evenly with an offset spatula. Run the spatula along the sides of the cake while turning the cake stand or cake turntable (if using) to achieve an even finish.

11. Using the dark green frosting, pipe a line around the cake that is about ½ inch up from the bottom. Pipe a hexagon pattern on the shell using the darker green frosting, continuing the pattern until it meets the border you just piped (see note on opposite page).

12. Press the marshmallow treat head, limbs, and tail into the cake. For the eyes, press the points of the two chocolate chips into the top of the head and dab a small amount of white candy melts in the upper corner of each chocolate chip, if desired.

13. Using a toothpick and the melted chocolate chips, dab on a smile.

14. Microwave the fruit-flavored candy chew for 5 seconds to soften it, and then mold a small portion of it into two ovals for cheeks. Press the cheeks on the sides of the face, beside the eyes.

To pipe the hexagon pattern, start at the top of the shell and work in concentric circles downward. This method will make it easier to keep the pattern straight. But if you get confused along the way, don't sweat it. As long as you pipe geometric shapes, it will still look like a turtle shell. Nature isn't perfect, after all!

GIANT POPSICLE CAKE

I've never been a fruit popsicle kind of girl. Fruit popsicles are light, refreshing, and reminiscent of something healthy. As a kid, I preferred those that were rich, decadent, and reminiscent of something you would make if you hadn't eaten dessert for years. Since then, my taste buds have developed to appreciate a balance between the two, and this cake is a reflection of that. Studded with sweet-tart raspberries and flavored with bright lemon zest, it's fresh and indulgent at once.

FOR THE CAKE

Cooking spray

1½ cups fresh raspberries

1 tablespoon all-purpose flour

3 cups cake flour

2 cups sugar

2 teaspoons baking powder

½ teaspoon baking soda

1 teaspoon table salt

½ cup (1 stick) unsalted butter, cut into ½-inch cubes, at room temperature

4 large eggs, at room temperature

1 cup buttermilk, at room temperature

½ cup canola oil

4 teaspoons vanilla extract

2 tablespoons grated lemon zest

FOR THE FROSTING

1½ cups (3 sticks) unsalted butter, at room temperature

4½ cups confectioners' sugar

1½ teaspoons vanilla extract

3 tablespoons milk

Pink gel food color

FOR THE CHOCOLATE GANACHE

½ cup heavy whipping cream

1 cup semisweet chocolate chips

1. **MAKE THE CAKE:** Preheat the oven to 350°F. Spray a 9 x 13-inch baking pan with cooking spray and line it with parchment paper so it overhangs the sides to make the cake easier to remove. Spray the parchment again and clip the overhang in place on the sides of the pan using plain metal binder clips.

2. In a small bowl, toss the raspberries with the all-purpose flour until the berries are fully coated. Set aside.

3. In a stand mixer fitted with the paddle attachment, combine the cake flour, sugar, baking powder, baking soda, and salt on low speed until well mixed, about 1 minute. With the mixer running on low speed, add the cubed butter and beat until the mixture resembles coarse sand, about 4 minutes. (For more on this technique, see page 23.)

4. In a separate bowl, whisk together the eggs, buttermilk, oil, vanilla, and lemon zest. With the mixer running on low speed, gradually add the wet ingredients to the dry ingredients and beat just until combined. Using a rubber spatula, fold in the raspberries. Pour the batter into the prepared pan.

5. Bake until a toothpick inserted into the center of the cake comes out clean, 30 to 35 minutes. Let the cake cool for 10 minutes in the pan. Then use the parchment paper to transfer the cake to a wire rack and let it cool completely. If necessary, use a serrated knife or a cake leveler to level the top of the cake.

6. **MAKE THE FROSTING:** In a stand mixer fitted with the paddle attachment, beat the butter on high speed until smooth, about 1 minute. Reduce the speed to low, gradually add the confectioners' sugar, and beat until combined. Beat in the vanilla and milk until combined. Scrape down the sides of the bowl. Beat the frosting on medium-high speed until it is light and fluffy, about 3 minutes.

7. Transfer 1 tablespoon of the frosting to a small plastic zip-top bag and cut off a small tip.

8. Dye the remaining frosting pink with the pink gel food color and transfer it to a piping bag or a large plastic zip-top bag. Cut off a large tip.

9. **MAKE THE CHOCOLATE GANACHE:** In a glass measuring cup or a microwave-safe bowl, microwave the heavy whipping cream in 30-second intervals until it begins to simmer, stirring after each interval. Carefully add the chocolate chips and let the mixture sit for 5 minutes. Stir until it is smooth and let it cool slightly. Transfer the ganache to a piping bag and cut off a small tip.

10. **DECORATE THE CAKE:** Pipe a small circle of white frosting on the upper corner of each of the chocolate candy melts for pupils.

11. If you are using the pink fruit-flavored candy chew, microwave it for 5 seconds to soften it, and then mold a small portion of it into two ovals for cheeks.

(recipe and ingredients continue)

CAKES

2 chocolate candy melts

1 pink fruit-flavored candy chew, such as Starburst, or 2 pink jelly beans

Rainbow sprinkles

1 graham cracker

12. Cut the top portion of the cake into a curve to mimic a popsicle shape (and discard the trimmed-off cake piece).

13. For the crumb coat, pipe a thin layer of pink frosting over the entire cake and spread it evenly with an offset spatula. Refrigerate the cake for 15 minutes.

14. Pipe pink frosting over the entire cake and spread it evenly around the sides of the cake with an offset spatula. Using the offset spatula, bring the frosting from the top edges of the cake toward the center to create a flat top.

15. Using the ganache, practice piping a smile on a sheet of parchment paper to ensure that the ganache is cool enough to pipe. If it's still too runny, let it sit at room temperature for about 3 more minutes, or until piping is successful. Then pipe a smile on the lower third of the cake. Place an eye on each side of the smile, and then place the fruit-flavored candy chew or the pink jelly bean cheeks next to the eyes.

16. Using a toothpick, lightly draw the outline of the chocolate drip on the top portion of the cake. Cut a larger tip for the chocolate ganache, and then pipe the ganache into the outlined area. Use an offset spatula to spread the ganache evenly. Sprinkle rainbow sprinkles on top.

17. Using a serrated knife, cut one edge of the graham cracker into a curve. Cut a slit in the bottom side of the cake and press the graham cracker into it to make the popsicle stick.

AVOCADO CAKE

MAKES ONE
9 X 13-INCH
CAKE

Recently, it seems that avocados have absolutely exploded in popularity, and for a good reason. They're the perfect light but creamy addition to a salad, sandwich, or slice of toast. And if we shape a cake like an avocado, it still counts as "good fats," right? Actually, maybe don't answer that. But do enjoy this adorable cake that's an homage to one of nature's best foods!

FOR THE CAKE

Cooking spray

3 cups cake flour

2 cups sugar

2 teaspoons baking powder

½ teaspoon baking soda

1 teaspoon table salt

½ cup (1 stick) unsalted butter, cut into ½-inch cubes, at room temperature

4 large eggs, at room temperature

1 cup buttermilk, at room temperature

½ cup canola oil

4 teaspoons vanilla extract

FOR THE FROSTING

1½ cups (3 sticks) unsalted butter, at room temperature

4½ cups confectioners' sugar

1½ teaspoons vanilla extract

3 tablespoons milk

1 tablespoon natural unsweetened cocoa powder

Green, yellow, and black gel food colors

1. MAKE THE CAKE: Preheat the oven to 350°F. Spray a 9 x 13-inch baking pan with cooking spray and line it with parchment paper so it overhangs the sides to make the cake easier to remove. Spray the parchment again and clip the overhang in place on the sides of the pan using plain metal binder clips.

2. In a stand mixer fitted with the paddle attachment, combine the cake flour, sugar, baking powder, baking soda, and salt on low speed until well mixed, about 1 minute. With the mixer running on low speed, add the cubed butter and beat until the mixture resembles coarse sand, about 4 minutes. (For more on this technique, see page 23.)

3. In a separate bowl, whisk together the eggs, buttermilk, oil, and vanilla. With the mixer running on low speed, gradually add the wet ingredients to the dry ingredients and beat just until combined. Pour the batter into the prepared pan.

4. Bake until a toothpick inserted into the center of the cake comes out clean, 30 to 35 minutes. Let the cake

cool in the pan for 10 minutes. Then use the parchment paper to transfer the cake to a wire rack and let it cool completely. If necessary, use a serrated knife or a cake leveler to level the cake.

5. MAKE THE FROSTING: In a stand mixer fitted with the paddle attachment, beat the butter on high speed until smooth, about 1 minute. Reduce the speed to low, gradually add the confectioners' sugar, and beat until combined. Beat in the vanilla and milk until combined. Scrape down the sides of the bowl. Beat the frosting on medium-high speed until it is light and fluffy, about 3 minutes. Transfer ⅓ cup of the frosting to a separate bowl and stir in the cocoa powder.

6. Transfer 1 teaspoon of the chocolate frosting to a separate bowl and color it with the black gel food color. Transfer the black frosting to a small plastic zip-top bag and cut off a small tip.

7. Transfer the remaining chocolate frosting to a plastic zip-top bag and cut off a medium tip.

(recipe and ingredients continue)

1 pink fruit-flavored candy chew,
such as Starburst

2 white confetti quin

8. Dye the remaining frosting lime green with equal amounts of green and yellow food colors. Transfer it to a piping bag or a large plastic zip-top bag and cut off a large tip.

9. DECORATE THE CAKE: Using a serrated knife, cut the cake into an avocado shape. For the crumb coat, spread a thin layer of the lime green frosting over the entire cake. Refrigerate the cake for 15 minutes.

10. Pipe lime green frosting over the entire cake and spread it evenly around the sides of the cake with an offset spatula. Use the offset spatula to bring the frosting from the top edges of the cake toward the center to create a flat top.

11. Dye the remaining lime green frosting a darker green with more green gel food color. Transfer the darker green frosting to a piping bag and pipe a thin border around the top edge of the cake. Using the offset spatula, smooth the frosting to blend it in with the lighter lime green frosting, working both toward the center of the cake and down the sides.

12. Pipe the brown chocolate frosting in the center of the cake to create the avocado pit and gently smooth it with an offset spatula.

13. Pipe the eyes and smile onto the avocado pit with the black frosting. Press one white confetti quin in the upper corner of each eye for a pupil.

14. Microwave the pink fruit-flavored candy chew for 5 seconds to soften it, and then mold a small portion of it into two ovals for cheeks. Place the cheeks beside the eyes.

BUBBLE TEA CAKE

MAKES
ONE 6-INCH
LAYER CAKE

How do you like your bubble tea: 25 percent sweet? 50 percent ice? Boba or no boba? This cold, refreshing milky tea is originally from Taiwan, and the tapioca pearls—the boba—that collect in the bottom of your cup gave it its name. However you order your tea, I can promise you that this cake is 100 percent tasty and 100 percent cute, and looks just like the real thing. You can buy bubble tea straws online, or grab an extra the next time you go to your local boba tea place.

FOR THE CAKE

Cooking spray

3 cups cake flour

2 cups sugar

2 teaspoons baking powder

½ teaspoon baking soda

1 teaspoon table salt

½ cup (1 stick) unsalted butter, cut into ½-inch cubes, at room temperature

4 large eggs, at room temperature

1 cup buttermilk, at room temperature

½ cup canola oil

4 teaspoons vanilla extract

1. MAKE THE CAKE: Preheat the oven to 350°F. Spray three 6-inch round cake pans with cooking spray. Line the pans with parchment paper and lightly spray again.

2. In a stand mixer fitted with the paddle attachment, combine the cake flour, sugar, baking powder, baking soda, and salt on low speed until well mixed, about 1 minute. With the mixer running on low speed, add the cubed butter and beat until the mixture resembles coarse sand, about 4 minutes. (For more on this technique, see page 23.)

FOR THE FROSTING

1½ cups (3 sticks) unsalted butter, at room temperature

4½ cups confectioners' sugar

1½ teaspoons vanilla extract

3 tablespoons milk

Black, purple, and pink gel food color

FOR THE DECORATIONS

About 1 cup brown candy-coated chocolate peanut candies, such as Peanut M&M's

2 chocolate candy melts

2 pink jelly beans

About ½ cup mini marshmallows

1 bubble tea straw

3. In a separate bowl, whisk together the eggs, buttermilk, oil, and vanilla. With the mixer running on low speed, gradually add the wet ingredients to the dry ingredients and beat just until combined. Divide the batter evenly among the prepared pans.

4. Bake until a toothpick inserted into the centers of the cakes comes out clean, 35 to 40 minutes. Let the cakes cool in the pans for 10 minutes. Then run a knife around the edges of the pans and turn the cakes out onto a cooling rack. Peel off the parchment paper and let them cool completely.

5. MAKE THE FROSTING: In a stand mixer fitted with the paddle attachment, beat the butter on high speed until smooth, about 1 minute. Reduce the speed to low, gradually add the confectioners' sugar, and beat until combined. Beat in the vanilla and milk until combined. Scrape down the sides of the bowl. Beat the frosting on medium-high speed until it is light and fluffy, about 3 minutes.

6. Transfer 1 tablespoon of the frosting to a separate bowl and color it black with the black gel food coloring. Transfer it to a small piping bag or to a small plastic zip-top bag and cut off a small tip.

7. Transfer another tablespoon of the frosting to a small piping bag or to a small plastic zip-top bag and cut off a small tip.

8. Dye the remaining frosting lilac using the purple gel food color and a small amount of pink gel food color. Transfer the lilac frosting to a piping bag or to a large plastic zip-top bag and cut off a medium tip.

9. DECORATE THE CAKE: Using a cake leveler or a serrated knife, cut the rounded tops off the cakes. Pipe about 1 tablespoon of the lilac frosting onto a 6-inch cake board, and place one cake layer on top. Pipe a layer of lilac frosting onto the cake and spread it evenly with an offset spatula. Place another cake layer on top, pipe on a layer of lilac frosting, and spread the frosting evenly with an offset spatula. Top with the final cake layer, placing the cut side down. For the crumb coat, pipe a thin layer of lilac frosting over the entire cake and spread it evenly with an offset spatula. Refrigerate the cake for 15 minutes.

10. Pipe lilac frosting over the entire cake and spread it evenly with an offset spatula. Run an icing smoother over the sides of the cake to smooth the frosting. Using an offset spatula, bring the frosting from the top edges of the cake toward the center to create a flat top.

11. For the tapioca pearls, place the chocolate-covered peanut candies around the bottom third of the cake, spacing them out randomly on the frosting.

12. Pipe a circle of the white frosting on the upper corners of each of the chocolate candy melts for the eyes.

13. Using the black frosting, pipe a smile onto the front of the cake above the tapioca pearls. Press the eyes on each side of the smile, and then add the pink jelly beans beside the eyes.

14. Press the mini marshmallows around the top of the cake, right on the edge, to mimic the lid of a cup, and then stick the straw into the top of the cake.

PANDA CAKE

MAKES
ONE 6-INCH
LAYER CAKE

Pandas are the quintessential kawaii animal. With their big eyes and fluffy bodies, you just want to reach out and give them a big hug. But because a trip to China to see real-life pandas isn't in the books for now, I decided to create the next best thing: a cake decorated like a panda! For this one, I used my favorite chocolate cake recipe. In fact, it's become tradition in our family that every April 24—my birthday—I make and devour an entire chocolate cake by myself. Okay, let me clarify—not in *one* sitting, and my dad will usually have a few slices, but for the most part I take down the whole thing. And my cake of choice is the one used in this recipe. It's rich, fluffy, moist, and absolutely divine when paired with a creamy buttercream frosting.

FOR THE CAKE

Cooking spray

1½ cups all-purpose flour

1½ cups sugar

⅔ cup natural unsweetened
cocoa powder

1½ teaspoons baking soda

¾ teaspoon baking powder

1 teaspoon table salt

2 large eggs, at room temperature

¾ cup buttermilk,
at room temperature

6 tablespoons canola oil

1 teaspoon vanilla extract

¾ cup hot coffee

FOR THE FROSTING

1½ cups (3 sticks) unsalted butter,
at room temperature

4½ cups confectioners' sugar

1½ teaspoons vanilla extract

3 tablespoons milk

Black and pink gel food colors

1. **MAKE THE CAKE:** Preheat the oven to 350°F. Spray three 6-inch round cake pans with cooking spray. Line the pans with parchment paper and lightly spray again.

2. In a large bowl, whisk together the flour, sugar, cocoa powder, baking soda, baking powder, and salt. Add the eggs, buttermilk, oil, and vanilla. Using a handheld electric mixer, beat on medium speed until combined. Pour in the hot coffee and beat on medium speed until just combined. Divide the batter among the prepared pans.

3. Bake until a toothpick inserted into the centers of the cakes comes out clean, 27 to 30 minutes. Let the cakes cool in the pans for 10 minutes. Then run a knife around the edges of the pans and turn the cakes out onto a cooling rack. Peel off the parchment paper and let them cool completely.

4. **MAKE THE FROSTING:** In a stand mixer fitted with the paddle attachment, beat the butter on high speed until smooth, about 1 minute. Reduce the speed to low and gradually add the confectioners' sugar. Add in the vanilla and milk and beat until combined. Using a rubber spatula, scrape down the sides of the bowl. Beat the frosting on medium-high speed until it is smooth and fluffy, about 3 minutes.

5. Transfer 1 tablespoon of the frosting to a small plastic zip-top bag and cut off a small tip.

6. Transfer 1 tablespoon of the frosting to a separate bowl and color it black with the black gel food color. Transfer it to a small plastic zip-top bag and cut off a small tip.

7. Transfer ½ cup of the frosting to a separate bowl and color it pink with the pink gel food color. Transfer it to a small plastic zip-top bag and cut off a small tip.

8. Transfer the remaining frosting to a piping bag or a large plastic zip-top bag and cut off a large tip.

(recipe and ingredients continue)

Refrigerating the cake before smoothing the scallops allows you to touch them up without distorting their shape. Don't skip this step!

Rainbow sprinkle mix

4 chocolate sandwich cookies, such as Oreos

2 pink jelly beans

9. DECORATE THE CAKE: Using a cake leveler or a serrated knife, cut the rounded tops off the cakes. Pipe about 1 tablespoon of the remaining white frosting onto a 6-inch cake board, and then place one cake layer on top. Pipe a layer of white frosting onto the cake and spread it evenly with an offset spatula. Place a cake layer on top, pipe on a layer of white frosting, and spread it evenly with an offset spatula. Top with the final cake layer, cut-side down. For the crumb coat, pipe a thin layer of white frosting over the entire cake and spread it evenly with an offset spatula (see photos 1, 2, and 3). Refrigerate the cake for 15 minutes.

10. Pipe white frosting over the entire cake and spread it evenly with an offset spatula (see photo 4). Run an icing smoother around the sides of the cake to smooth the frosting (see photo 5). Using an offset spatula, bring the frosting from the top edges of the cake toward the center to create a flat top (see photo 6).

11. Using the reserved pink frosting, pipe the outline of a scallop border around the top edge of the cake. Then fill in the scallops with more pink frosting, and pipe pink frosting

to cover the top of the cake as well. Refrigerate the cake until the frosting is firm and doesn't stick to your finger when tapped, about 20 minutes.

12. Using an offset spatula, carefully smooth the scallops and the top of the cake (see photo 7). Press the rainbow sprinkles over the pink frosting.

13. For the ears, use a serrated knife to cut off about ⅛ inch from the bottom of two of the chocolate sandwich cookies to create a flat edge. Place the ears on top of the cake toward the front (see photo 8).

14. Separate the two remaining chocolate sandwich cookies and scrape off the cream filling. Use a serrated knife to cut two of the chocolate cookies into ovals for eyes, and cut a third chocolate cookie into a triangle for a nose. (You can eat the remaining cookie!) Using the reserved white frosting, pipe dots onto the eyes for pupils.

15. Press the eyes and nose onto the front of the cake (see photo 9); use the reserved black frosting to pipe on a smile. Press a pink jelly bean on each side of the eyes for cheeks.

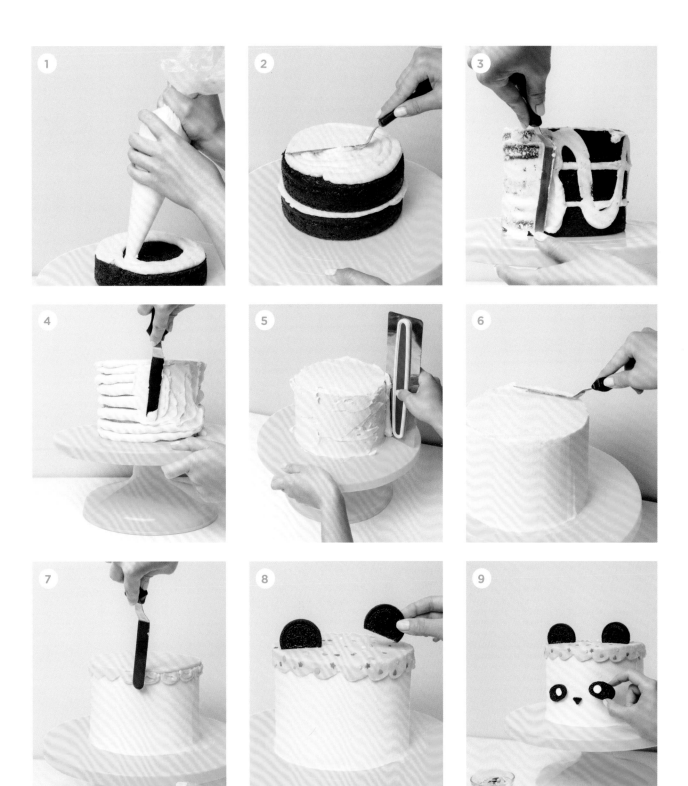

Cream cheese frosting tends to be softer than American buttercream, which makes it slightly trickier to use for frosting layer cakes. Be gentle when applying the crumb coat, and then let the cake chill in the fridge for at least 30 minutes—you want it good and firm before applying the final layer. If your frosting is too thin, refrigerate it for 30 minutes and then proceed with the decorating.

BUNNY CARROT CAKE

MAKES
ONE 6-INCH
LAYER CAKE

This cake is dedicated to my childhood favorite stuffed animal, whom I nonsensically (but affectionately) named "Bunny Bunskins." Much like this adorable cake, Bunny Bunskins had long pink ears and a sweet smile. And because her favorite food was carrots, I had to make this a carrot cake!

Carrot cake is one of the first recipes my mom taught me to make, and it's still one of my favorites. At nine years old, I was still struggling to remember that "7 times 4 equals 28," but I could use a food processor to finely grate carrots and turn out tasty cakes for my family. I've even made carrot cake for my friends at college!

FOR THE CAKE
Cooking spray

2 cups all-purpose flour

1 teaspoon baking powder

¾ teaspoon baking soda

1 tablespoon ground cinnamon

½ teaspoon ground nutmeg

⅛ teaspoon ground cloves

1 teaspoon table salt

3 large eggs, at room temperature

¾ cup granulated sugar

¾ cup (packed) light brown sugar

1 cup canola oil

3 cups peeled and grated carrots

FOR THE FROSTING
12 ounces cream cheese, at room temperature

¾ cup (1½ sticks) unsalted butter, at room temperature

6 cups confectioners' sugar

2 teaspoons vanilla extract

Black gel food color

1. MAKE THE CAKE: Preheat the oven to 350°F. Spray three 6-inch round cake pans with cooking spray. Line the pans with parchment paper and lightly spray again.

2. In a large bowl, whisk together the flour, baking powder, baking soda, cinnamon, nutmeg, cloves, and salt.

3. In a stand mixer fitted with the whisk attachment, combine the eggs, granulated sugar, and brown sugar and beat on medium speed until frothy, about 1 minute. Reduce the speed to low, slowly pour in the canola oil, and beat until combined. Using a rubber spatula, fold in the dry ingredients until combined, and then fold in the carrots. Divide the batter evenly among the prepared pans.

4. Bake until a toothpick inserted into the centers of the cakes comes out clean, 35 to 40 minutes. Let the cakes cool in the pans for 10 minutes. Then run a knife around the edges of the pans and turn the cakes out onto a cooling rack. Peel off the parchment paper and let them cool completely.

5. MAKE THE FROSTING: In a stand mixer fitted with the paddle attachment, combine the cream cheese and butter and beat on medium speed until smooth, about 2 minutes. Beat in the confectioners' sugar gradually, and then beat in the vanilla. Scrape down the sides of the bowl. Beat the frosting on medium-high speed until it is light and fluffy, about 2 minutes.

6. Transfer 1 tablespoon of the frosting to a separate bowl and color it black with the black gel food coloring. Transfer the black frosting to a small piping bag or a small plastic zip-top bag and cut off a small tip. Transfer the remaining frosting to a piping bag or large plastic zip-top bag and cut off a large tip.

7. DECORATE THE CAKE: Using a cake leveler or a serrated knife, cut the rounded tops off the cakes. Pipe about 1 tablespoon of the white frosting onto a 6-inch cake board, then place one cake layer on top. Pipe a layer of white frosting onto the cake and spread it evenly with an offset spatula. Place another cake layer on top, pipe on a layer of white frosting, and spread the frosting evenly with an offset spatula. Top with the final cake layer, placing the cut side down. For the crumb coat,

(recipe and ingredients continue)

4 ounces white candy coating, melted
(about ¼ cup melted coating)

2 chocolate candy melts

3 ounces pink candy coating, melted
(about 3 tablespoons melted
coating)

1 chocolate chip

2 pink jelly beans

Confetti quins

pipe a thin layer of white frosting over
the entire cake and spread it evenly
with an offset spatula. Refrigerate the
cake for 30 minutes.

8. Pipe white frosting over the entire
cake and spread it evenly with an
offset spatula. Run an icing smoother
around the sides of the cake to smooth
the frosting. Using an offset spatula,
bring the frosting from the top edges
of the cake toward the center to create
a flat top.

9. Dab a small amount of the white
candy coating in the upper corner of
each chocolate candy melt for a pupil.
Let it set completely, about 10 minutes.

10. To make the inner parts of the ears,
place a sheet of parchment paper over
the template (see page 230). Spoon the
melted pink candy coating over the
parchment and spread it out according
to the template to make the inner
portion of the ears. Let the coating
set completely at room temperature,

about 15 minutes. Finish the ears by
spooning the remaining melted white
candy coating over the pink, covering
the back side completely. Spread out
the candy coating according to the
template. Let it set completely at room
temperature, about 15 minutes.

11. Press the side of the chocolate
chip into the front of the cake for a
nose, and then place the eyes on both
sides.

12. Press a pink jelly bean on each side
of the cake, beside the eyes.

13. Pipe a mouth under the nose with
the reserved black icing.

14. Gently remove the ears from the
parchment paper. Use a knife to make
two slits in the top of the cake as a
guide for the ear placement, then
carefully place one ear into each
slit. Sprinkle a ring of confetti quins
around the outside edge of the top of
the cake.

SUCCULENT CUPCAKES

In my first year of college, I developed a love for cute, stylish succulents because they're so easy to grow and care for. If only a good GPA were as easy to maintain! These fun cupcakes look like little planters of the desert plants. I made only two types of succulents here, but there are so many others out there you can make, too—feel free to experiment with the meringues.

FOR THE MERINGUES

2 large egg whites

¼ teaspoon vanilla extract

Pinch of cream of tartar

Pinch of salt

½ cup sugar

Green and yellow gel food colors

White jimmies

White nonpareils

Flower sprinkles

Black decorating icing, fitted with a small round tip (I like Wilton brand)

FOR THE CUPCAKES

2 cups all-purpose flour

2 cups sugar

¾ cup natural unsweetened cocoa powder

2 teaspoons baking soda

1 teaspoon baking powder

1 teaspoon table salt

2 large eggs, at room temperature

1 cup buttermilk, at room temperature

½ cup canola oil

1. MAKE THE MERINGUES: Preheat the oven to 225°F. Line a baking sheet with parchment paper.

2. In a stand mixer fitted with the whisk attachment, combine the egg whites, vanilla, cream of tartar, and salt and beat on medium speed until foamy, about 1 minute. With the mixer running on low speed, gradually add the sugar. Increase the speed to high and beat until stiff, glossy peaks form, about 7 minutes. Add in equal amounts of green and yellow gel food colors to dye the mixture lime green and beat to combine.

3. Place half of the mixture into a piping bag fitted with a medium star tip and the other half into a piping bag with a medium tip.

4. For the round "blob" succulents, use the piping bag with the star tip. Holding it vertically with the star tip directly over the prepared baking sheet, squeeze out a dollop of the meringue mixture.

5. For the cacti, use either piping bag to pipe the meringue mixture onto the prepared baking sheet, first piping the center stem, followed by the arms.

6. Sprinkle white jimmies over half of the meringues, and sprinkle white nonpareils over the other half. Add flower sprinkles as desired for accents.

7. Bake the meringues until they can be removed from the parchment paper without leaving any residue, about 1 hour and 30 minutes. Let them cool for 10 minutes on the baking sheet. Then lift them off the parchment and transfer them to a wire rack and let them cool completely.

8. Pipe on faces with the black decorating icing.

9. MAKE THE CUPCAKES: Preheat the oven to 350°F. Line two 12-cup cupcake tins with liners.

10. In a large bowl, whisk together the flour, sugar, cocoa powder, baking soda, baking powder, and salt. Add the eggs, buttermilk, oil, and vanilla. Using a handheld electric mixer, beat on medium speed until combined. Pour in the hot coffee and beat on medium speed until just combined. Divide the batter among the lined cupcake cups, filling them about three-fourths of the way.

(recipe and ingredients continue)

1 teaspoon vanilla extract

1 cup hot coffee

FOR THE VANILLA FROSTING

1 cup (2 sticks) unsalted butter,
    at room temperature

3 cups confectioners' sugar

1 teaspoon vanilla extract

2 tablespoons milk

FOR THE DECORATIONS

1 cup graham cracker crumbs (from
    about 6 to 7 graham crackers)

Flower sprinkles

11. Bake until a toothpick inserted into the center of the cupcakes comes out clean, 18 to 20 minutes. Let the cupcakes cool in the tins for 5 minutes. Then turn them out onto a wire rack and let them cool completely.

12. MAKE THE FROSTING: In a stand mixer fitted with the paddle attachment, beat the butter on high speed until smooth, about 1 minute. Reduce the speed to low, gradually add the confectioners' sugar, and beat until combined. Beat in the vanilla and milk until combined. Scrape down the sides of the bowl. Beat the frosting on medium-high speed until it is light and fluffy, about 3 minutes.

13. DECORATE THE CUPCAKES: Place the graham cracker crumbs in a shallow bowl.

14. Using an offset spatula, spread about 1 tablespoon of the frosting onto each cupcake. Press the tops of the cupcakes in the graham cracker crumbs to create the "sand." Place the succulent meringues on the cupcakes, pressing them into the frosting. For extra stability, use a knife to make a slit in each cupcake and insert the standing cacti in the slit. Decorate the cupcakes with additional flower sprinkles.

RACCOON CUPCAKES

As it turns out, raccoons love my baking. I know this because my family had to affix industrial-strength black straps across our compost bins so that the creatures can no longer knock over our garbage to dig around for kawaii sweet treats. Sorry, guys—this dessert is for you! Well, figuratively that is.

FOR THE CUPCAKES

2 cups all-purpose flour

2 cups sugar

¾ cup natural unsweetened cocoa powder

2 teaspoons baking soda

1 teaspoon baking powder

1 teaspoon table salt

2 large eggs, at room temperature

1 cup buttermilk, at room temperature

½ cup canola oil

1 teaspoon vanilla extract

1 cup hot coffee

1. MAKE THE CUPCAKES: Preheat the oven to 350°F. Line two 12-cup cupcake tins with liners.

2. In a large bowl, whisk together the flour, sugar, cocoa powder, baking soda, baking powder, and salt. Add the eggs, buttermilk, oil, and vanilla. Using a handheld electric mixer, beat on medium speed until combined. Pour in the hot coffee and beat on medium speed until just combined. Divide the batter among the lined cupcake cups, filling them about three-fourths of the way.

3. Bake until a toothpick inserted into the center of the cupcakes comes out clean, 18 to 20 minutes. Let the cupcakes cool in the tins for 5 minutes. Then turn them out onto a wire rack and let them cool completely.

4. MAKE THE FROSTING: In a stand mixer fitted with the paddle attachment, beat the butter on high speed until smooth, about 1 minute. Reduce the speed to low, gradually add the confectioners' sugar and cocoa powder, and beat until combined. Scrape down the sides of the bowl. Add the milk, vanilla, and espresso powder, if using, and beat on low speed until combined. Increase the speed to high and beat until the frosting is smooth and fluffy, about 2 minutes.

(recipe and ingredients continue)

FOR THE FROSTING

1½ cups (3 sticks) unsalted butter, at room temperature

4 cups confectioners' sugar

¾ cup natural unsweetened cocoa powder

⅓ cup milk

1 teaspoon vanilla extract

1 teaspoon instant espresso powder (optional)

FOR THE DECORATIONS

4 ounces chocolate candy coating, melted (about ¼ cup chocolate candy coating)

48 brown candy-coated chocolates, such as M&M's

24 white chocolate chips

3 tablespoons white chocolate chips, melted

Pink confetti quins

5. DECORATE THE CUPCAKES: Place a sheet of parchment paper over the raccoon eye template (see page 235). Spoon or pipe the melted chocolate candy coating over the template for the raccoon eyes. Let it set completely at room temperature, about 10 minutes. (Reserve the excess chocolate candy coating.)

6. Using an offset spatula, spread about 1½ tablespoons of the frosting on each cupcake and create a flat top. Clean off the spatula by scraping any excess frosting back into the frosting bowl, and then run the spatula at a 45-degree angle along the sides of each cupcake to create a flat edge.

7. Place a candy-coated chocolate on each side of the cupcake for ears.

8. Gently remove the raccoon eye bases from the parchment paper and place them flat-side up on the center of each cupcake.

9. Press the point of a white chocolate chip into the center of each cupcake, just below the eye base, for a nose.

10. Place the melted white chocolate in a small plastic zip-top bag, cut off a small tip, and pipe small circles for the raccoon eye whites. Let set completely, about 10 minutes.

11. Remelt the reserved chocolate candy coating if necessary, and then pipe a dot of the melted coating in the upper corner of each eye white for pupils and an oval on the white chocolate chip nose. Let set completely, about 5 minutes.

12. Using tweezers, place a pink confetti quin on either side of the eyes for cheeks.

COCONUT BEAR CUPCAKES

**MAKES
2 DOZEN
CUPCAKES**

One of my favorite parts of kawaii style is the way it can turn even seemingly "scary" animals into cute, approachable balls of fluff. These cupcakes are a stellar example of this phenomenon. A bear in real life? I'd run the other way. A bear made of moist, tender vanilla cake and mounds of coconut? Almost too cute to "bear!"

FOR THE CUPCAKES

3 cups cake flour

2 cups sugar

2 teaspoons baking powder

½ teaspoon baking soda

1 teaspoon table salt

½ cup (1 stick) butter, cut into ½-inch cubes, at room temperature

4 large eggs, at room temperature

1 cup buttermilk, at room temperature

½ cup canola oil

4 teaspoons vanilla extract

FOR THE FROSTING

1 cup (2 sticks) unsalted butter, at room temperature

3 cups confectioners' sugar

1 teaspoon vanilla extract

2 tablespoons milk

1. **MAKE THE CUPCAKES:** Preheat the oven to 350°F. Line two 12-cup cupcake tins with liners.

2. In a stand mixer fitted with the paddle attachment, combine the cake flour, sugar, baking powder, baking soda, and salt on low speed until well mixed, about 1 minute. With the mixer running on low speed, add the cubed butter and beat until the mixture resembles coarse sand, about 4 minutes. (For more on this technique, see page 23.)

3. In a separate bowl, whisk together the eggs, buttermilk, oil, and vanilla. With the mixer running on low speed, gradually add the wet ingredients to the dry ingredients and beat just until combined. Divide the batter among the lined cupcake cups, filling them about two-thirds of the way.

4. Bake until a toothpick inserted into the center of the cupcakes comes out clean, 16 to 18 minutes. Let the cupcakes cool in the tins for 5 minutes. Then turn them out onto a wire rack and let them cool completely.

5. **MAKE THE FROSTING:** In a stand mixer fitted with the paddle attachment, beat the butter on high speed until smooth, about 1 minute. Reduce the speed to low, gradually add the confectioners' sugar, and beat until combined. Beat in the vanilla and milk until combined. Scrape down the sides of the bowl. Beat the frosting on medium-high speed until it is light and fluffy, about 3 minutes.

6. **DECORATE THE CUPCAKES:** Place ½ cup of the flaked coconut in a plastic zip-top bag and add a drop of pink gel food color. Shake the bag to distribute the color evenly, and add more food color if necessary to reach the desired shade of pink. Repeat, combining ½-cup portions of coconut with the yellow, purple, and blue food colors in separate bags. Place each color of coconut into a shallow bowl. Place the remaining ½ cup white coconut in a shallow bowl.

FOR THE DECORATIONS

2½ cups sweetened flaked coconut

Pink, yellow, purple, and blue gel food colors

12 mini marshmallows

2 tablespoons chocolate chips, melted

48 mini chocolate chips

10 candy melts in each color: white, pink, yellow, purple, and blue

7. Using an offset spatula, spread about 1 tablespoon of the frosting on each cupcake. Dip each cupcake into a different bowl of colored coconut for the bear fur.

8. Cut the mini marshmallows in half. Place the marshmallow halves on the lower third of the cupcakes to make the bears' muzzles.

9. Place the melted chocolate in a small plastic zip-top bag and cut off a small tip. Pipe the bears' mouths on top of the muzzles.

10. Press the point of a mini chocolate chip on each side of the mouth for eyes. Insert two candy melts of the corresponding color into the sides of the frosting for ears.

To make it easier to cut the white candy melts in half, dip your sharp knife in hot water between cuts.

UNICORN CUPCAKES

MAKES
2 DOZEN
CUPCAKES

I challenge you to search for "cute cake decorating ideas" on the internet without coming across a unicorn cake. There's good reason for this inevitability—they are fun, colorful, and whimsical. And once you throw in some kawaii cuteness, you really have something special! These cupcakes make for an eye-catching party centerpiece, yet they're simple enough for a beginner to create.

FOR THE CUPCAKES

3 cups cake flour

2 cups sugar

2 teaspoons baking powder

½ teaspoon baking soda

1 teaspoon table salt

½ cup (1 stick) butter, cut into ½-inch cubes, at room temperature

4 large eggs, at room temperature

1 cup buttermilk, at room temperature

½ cup canola oil

4 teaspoons vanilla extract

½ cup confetti quins

FOR THE FROSTING

1 cup (2 sticks) unsalted butter, at room temperature

3 cups confectioners' sugar

1 teaspoon vanilla extract

2 tablespoons milk

Black gel food color

1. MAKE THE CUPCAKES: Preheat the oven to 350°F. Line two 12-cup cupcake tins with liners.

2. In a stand mixer fitted with the paddle attachment, combine the cake flour, sugar, baking powder, baking soda, and salt on low speed until well mixed, about 1 minute. With the mixer running on low speed, add the cubed butter and combine until the mixture resembles coarse sand, about 4 minutes. (For more on this technique, see page 23.)

3. In a separate bowl, whisk together the eggs, buttermilk, oil, and vanilla. With the mixer running on low speed, gradually add the wet ingredients to the dry ingredients and beat just until combined. Using a rubber spatula, fold in the confetti quins. Divide the batter among the lined cupcake cups, filling them about two-thirds of the way.

4. Bake until a toothpick inserted into the center of the cupcakes comes out clean, 16 to 18 minutes. Let the cupcakes cool in the tins for 5 minutes. Then turn them out onto a wire rack and let them cool completely.

5. MAKE THE FROSTING: In a stand mixer fitted with the paddle attachment, beat the butter on high speed until smooth, about 1 minute. Reduce the speed to low, gradually add in the confectioners' sugar, and beat until combined. Beat in the vanilla and milk until combined. Scrape down the sides of the bowl. Beat the frosting on medium-high speed until it is light and fluffy, about 3 minutes.

6. Transfer 2 tablespoons of the frosting to a separate bowl and color it black with the black gel food color. Place the frosting in a small piping bag fitted with a small round piping tip.

7. DECORATE THE CUPCAKES: Using a sharp knife, cut each white candy melt in half.

8. Place ¼ cup of the flaked coconut in a plastic zip-top bag and add a drop of pink gel food color. Shake the bag to distribute the color evenly and add more food color if necessary to reach the desired shade of pink. Repeat, combining ¼-cup portions of the coconut with the orange, yellow, green, blue, and purple food colors in individual plastic bags. Place all the colored coconut in a medium bowl and toss with a fork to combine.

(recipe and ingredients continue)

FOR THE DECORATIONS

24 white candy melts

1½ cups sweetened flaked coconut

Pink, orange, yellow, green, blue, and purple gel food colors

24 cone-shaped corn chips, such as Bugles

9. Using an offset spatula, spread about 1½ tablespoons of the white frosting on each cupcake and create a flat top (see photo 1). Clean off the spatula by scraping any excess frosting back into the frosting bowl, and then run the spatula at a 45-degree angle along the sides of each cupcake to create a flat edge (see photo 2).

10. If desired, break ⅛ inch off the bottom of each corn chip to make the horn shorter and more proportional to the cupcake. Place a corn chip on the upper portion of each cupcake for a horn. Insert one halved candy melt on either side of the horn for ears (see photo 3). Press the colored coconut on the upper portion of the cupcake to create a mane, and then pipe on eyes with the reserved black frosting (see photos 4 and 5).

KOALA CUPCAKES

**MAKES
2 DOZEN
CUPCAKES**

I watched plenty of nature documentaries during my middle-school science career, and I will admit that my most salient memory is watching an adorable koala give its caretaker a big, endearing hug. I want one of those hugs! But until I can venture to someplace where there are cuddly koalas, these cupcakes are close enough.

FOR THE CUPCAKES

2 cups all-purpose flour

2 cups sugar

¾ cup natural unsweetened cocoa powder

2 teaspoons baking soda

1 teaspoon baking powder

1 teaspoon table salt

2 large eggs, at room temperature

1 cup buttermilk, at room temperature

½ cup canola oil

1 teaspoon vanilla extract

1 cup hot coffee

1. MAKE THE CUPCAKES: Preheat the oven to 350°F. Line two 12-cup cupcake tins with liners.

2. In a large bowl, whisk together the flour, sugar, cocoa powder, baking soda, baking powder, and salt. Add the eggs, buttermilk, oil, and vanilla. Using a handheld electric mixer, beat on medium speed until combined. Pour in the hot coffee and beat on medium speed until just combined. Divide the batter among the lined cupcake cups, filling them about three-fourths of the way.

3. Bake until a toothpick inserted into the center of the cupcakes comes out clean, 18 to 20 minutes. Let the cupcakes cool in the tins for 5 minutes. Then turn them out onto a wire rack and let them cool completely.

4. MAKE THE FROSTING: In a stand mixer fitted with the paddle attachment, beat the butter on high speed until smooth, about 1 minute. Reduce the speed to low, gradually add the confectioners' sugar, and beat

until combined. Beat in the vanilla and milk until combined. Scrape down the sides of the bowl. Beat the frosting on medium-high speed until it is light and fluffy, about 3 minutes.

5. Transfer 2 tablespoons of the frosting to a small piping bag fitted with a small round tip or to a plastic zip-top bag and cut off a small tip.

6. Color the remaining frosting gray with a small amount of black gel food color. Transfer 2 tablespoons of the gray frosting to a separate bowl and dye it black with more black gel food color. Transfer the black frosting to a small piping bag fitted with a small round tip.

7. DECORATE THE CUPCAKES: Using an offset spatula, spread about 1½ tablespoons of the gray frosting on each cupcake and create a flat top. Clean off the spatula by scraping any excess frosting back into the frosting bowl, and then run the spatula at a 45-degree angle along the sides of each cupcake to create a flat edge.

(recipe and ingredients continue)

FOR THE FROSTING

1 cup (2 sticks) unsalted butter, at room temperature

3 cups confectioners' sugar

1 teaspoon vanilla extract

2 tablespoons milk

Black gel food color

FOR THE DECORATIONS

48 pink candy melts

24 chocolate-covered espresso beans

48 chocolate chips

8. Place the remaining gray frosting in a piping bag fitted with a small round tip.

9. For each cupcake, press two pink candy melts on each side of the upper portion of the cupcake. Pipe a line of gray frosting on the outer rim of the candy melts to define the ears.

10. Place one chocolate-covered espresso bean in the center each cupcake for the nose, and then use the reserved black frosting to pipe a mouth.

11. Press the point of one chocolate chip into the cupcake on each side of the espresso bean to make the eyes. Pipe a dot of white frosting in the upper corner of the eyes for pupils.

WALRUS CUPCAKES

MAKES
2 DOZEN
CUPCAKES

Aquariums are amazing places. I've always loved ogling the adorable, tiny baby fishes and hated walking through those "underwater" hallways that surround you with sharks on all sides. I get shivers just thinking about those experiments in fear-tolerance. But you know what exhibit never gives anyone goosebumps? The walruses! They're so charming, I decided to create these fun double-chocolate cupcakes. With slivered almond tusks, they're an easy treat to whip up the next time you're craving a visit to the aquarium.

FOR THE CUPCAKES

2 cups all-purpose flour

2 cups sugar

¾ cup natural unsweetened cocoa powder

2 teaspoons baking soda

1 teaspoon baking powder

1 teaspoon table salt

2 large eggs, at room temperature

1 cup buttermilk, at room temperature

½ cup canola oil

1 teaspoon vanilla extract

1 cup hot coffee

FOR THE FROSTING

1½ cups (3 sticks) unsalted butter, at room temperature

4 cups confectioners' sugar

¾ cup natural unsweetened cocoa powder

⅓ cup milk

1 teaspoon vanilla extract

1 teaspoon instant espresso powder (optional)

FOR THE DECORATIONS

48 pieces of slivered almonds

72 mini semisweet chocolate chips

1. **MAKE THE CUPCAKES:** Preheat the oven to 350°F. Line two 12-cup cupcake tins with liners.

2. In a large bowl, whisk together the flour, sugar, cocoa powder, baking soda, baking powder, and salt. Add the eggs, buttermilk, oil, and vanilla. Using a handheld electric mixer, beat on medium speed until combined. Pour in the hot coffee and beat on medium speed until just combined. Divide the batter among the lined cupcake cups, filling them about three-fourths of the way.

3. Bake until a toothpick inserted into the center of the cupcakes comes out clean, 18 to 20 minutes. Let the cupcakes cool in the tins for 5 minutes. Then turn them out onto a wire rack and let them cool completely.

4. **MAKE THE FROSTING:** In a stand mixer fitted with the paddle attachment, beat the butter on high speed until smooth, about 1 minute. Reduce the speed to low, gradually add the confectioners' sugar and cocoa powder, and beat until combined. Scrape down the sides of the bowl. Add the milk, vanilla, and espresso powder if using, and beat on low speed until combined. Increase the speed to medium-high and beat until the frosting is smooth and fluffy, about 2 minutes.

5. **DECORATE THE CUPCAKES:** Using an offset spatula, spread about 1½ tablespoons of the frosting on each cupcake and create a flat top. Clean off the spatula by scraping any excess frosting back into the frosting bowl, and then run the spatula at a 45-degree angle along the sides of each cupcake to create a flat edge.

6. Place the remaining frosting in a piping bag fitted with a small round tip.

7. Pipe two circles next to each other on the lower third of the cupcakes to make the mouth. Insert a slivered almond into the bottom of each circle for tusks. Insert the tip of a mini chocolate chip into the top of the mouth for a nose.

8. Press the tip of a mini chocolate chip on each side of the mouth for eyes.

GINGERBREAD CUPCAKES

MAKES 1 DOZEN CUPCAKES

Am I the only one who is daunted at the prospect of decorating an entire gingerbread house? As a child, I was overwhelmed by the possibilities. Should I do a scalloped roof? Or is this more of a "shingled candy wafer" neighborhood? From the experience, I learned two things: I will never be an architect, and cupcakes are an easier and more manageable alternative. These moist, tender, beautifully spiced cupcakes are sure to please even the most conflicted decorator.

FOR THE CUPCAKES

1½ cups all-purpose flour

1 teaspoon baking soda

2 teaspoons ground cinnamon

2 teaspoons ground ginger

¼ teaspoon ground cloves

¼ teaspoon ground nutmeg

¼ teaspoon table salt

¼ cup (½ stick) unsalted butter, melted

1 large egg, at room temperature

½ cup canola oil

½ cup blackstrap molasses

½ cup (packed) light brown sugar

FOR THE FROSTING

4 ounces cream cheese, at room temperature

¼ cup (½ stick) unsalted butter, at room temperature

2 cups confectioners' sugar

½ teaspoon vanilla extract

2 teaspoons ground cinnamon

Brown gel food color

FOR THE DECORATIONS

Rainbow nonpareils

Confetti sprinkles

Large heart sprinkles

1. MAKE THE CUPCAKES: Preheat the oven to 350°F. Line a 12-cup cupcake tin with liners.

2. In a large bowl, whisk together the flour, baking soda, cinnamon, ginger, cloves, nutmeg, and salt.

3. In a separate bowl, whisk together the melted butter, egg, oil, molasses, brown sugar, and ½ cup of water. Pour the wet ingredients into the dry ingredients, and using a rubber spatula, fold until combined. Divide the batter among the lined cupcake cups, filling them about two-thirds of the way.

4. Bake until a toothpick inserted in the center of the cupcakes comes out clean, 19 to 22 minutes. Let the cupcakes cool in the tins for 5 minutes. Then turn them out onto a wire rack and let them cool completely.

5. MAKE THE FROSTING: In a stand mixer fitted with the paddle attachment, combine the cream cheese and butter and beat on medium speed until smooth. Add in the confectioners' sugar gradually, and beat until combined. Add in the vanilla and beat until combined. Scrape down the sides of the bowl. Beat the frosting on medium-high speed until it is light and fluffy, about 2 minutes.

6. Transfer ¼ cup of the frosting to a small piping bag fitted with a small round tip.

7. To the remaining frosting, add the cinnamon and enough brown gel food color to achieve a medium brown color.

8. DECORATE THE CUPCAKES: Using an offset spatula, spread about 1½ tablespoons of the brown frosting on each cupcake.

9. Pipe a decorative line along the top of the cupcakes with the white frosting, and sprinkle rainbow nonpareils on the piped lines.

10. Pipe a smile in the center of each cupcake with the white frosting, and place a confetti sprinkle on each side of the smile for the eyes.

11. On the lower portion of each cupcake, place two large heart sprinkles end-to-end to make a bow tie, or place them on the upper border for a bow. Place a confetti sprinkle in the center of the bow.

SHEEP CUPCAKES

MAKES 2 DOZEN CUPCAKES

If you've ever counted sheep to help fall asleep, these cupcakes are for you. I used to do the same thing! Unfortunately, I'm a very light sleeper and have previously counted to more than one hundred sheep before dozing off. So I wanted to make these cupcakes to recognize those patient fluffy creatures in my life. With mini marshmallow fur and chocolate chip eyes, these cupcakes are a sure ticket to sweet dreams.

FOR THE CUPCAKES

3 cups cake flour

2 cups sugar

2 teaspoons baking powder

½ teaspoon baking soda

1 teaspoon table salt

½ cup (1 stick) butter, cut into ½-inch cubes, at room temperature

4 large eggs, at room temperature

1 cup buttermilk, at room temperature

½ cup canola oil

4 teaspoons vanilla extract

FOR THE FROSTING

1 cup (2 sticks) unsalted butter, at room temperature

3 cups confectioners' sugar

1 teaspoon vanilla extract

2 tablespoons milk

Orange and yellow gel food color

FOR THE DECORATION

72 mini chocolate chips

3 cups mini marshmallows

48 whole unsalted cashews

1. MAKE THE CUPCAKES: Preheat the oven to 350°F. Line two 12-cup cupcake tins with liners.

2. In a stand mixer fitted with the paddle attachment, combine the cake flour, sugar, baking powder, baking soda, and salt on low speed until well mixed, about 1 minute. With the mixer running on low speed, add the cubed butter and beat until the mixture resembles coarse sand, about 4 minutes. (For more on this technique, see page 23.)

3. In a separate bowl, whisk together the eggs, buttermilk, oil, and vanilla. With the mixer running on low speed, gradually add the wet ingredients to the dry ingredients and beat just until combined. Divide the batter among the lined cupcake cups, filling them about two-thirds of the way.

4. Bake until a toothpick inserted into the center of the cupcakes comes out clean, 16 to 18 minutes. Let the cupcakes cool in the tins for 5 minutes. Then turn them out onto a wire rack and let them cool completely.

5. MAKE THE FROSTING: In a stand mixer fitted with the paddle attachment, beat the butter on high speed until smooth, about 1 minute. Reduce the speed to low, gradually add the confectioners' sugar, and beat until combined. Beat in the vanilla and milk until combined. Scrape down the sides of the bowl. Beat the frosting on medium-high speed until it is light and fluffy, about 3 minutes. Beat in a small amount of both orange and yellow gel food colors to create a flesh tone.

6. DECORATE THE CUPCAKES: Using an offset spatula, spread about 1½ tablespoons of the frosting on each cupcake. Insert one cashew on each side of the cupcakes to make the horns.

7. Cut the mini marshmallows in half. Arrange the halves, cut-sides down, on the cupcakes, leaving a small oval in the center on the bottom third for the face.

8. Place the side of one mini chocolate chip, with the point facing down, in the center of the oval for a nose, and then press the tip of a chocolate chip into the frosting on each side of the nose for eyes.

If the cream cheese frosting seems soft, resist the urge to add more confectioners' sugar. For this kind of frosting specifically, adding more sugar will not thicken it. Instead, refrigerate the frosting for 30 minutes, then stir it with a spatula and use it.

WATERMELON CUPCAKES

MAKES 15 CUPCAKES

While watermelon is a fantastic refreshing summertime fruit, it's a tricky one to bake with due to its light flavor and high water content. And since I've always loved red velvet cupcakes with their bright, eye-catching color, I decided to use them as the base for these cute cakes! And in fact, for every special occasion, my older brother, Chris, always requests these red velvet cupcakes. They really are tasty treats, particularly with their crown of cream cheese frosting.

FOR THE CUPCAKES

1¼ cups all-purpose flour

¼ cup natural unsweetened cocoa powder

½ teaspoon baking soda

¼ teaspoon table salt

½ cup (1 stick) unsalted butter, at room temperature

1 cup sugar

2 large eggs, at room temperature

½ cup sour cream, at room temperature

¼ cup milk, at room temperature

1 teaspoon vanilla extract

Red gel food color

FOR THE FROSTING

4 ounces cream cheese, at room temperature

¼ cup (½ stick) unsalted butter, at room temperature

2 cups confectioners' sugar

½ teaspoon vanilla extract

Green gel food color

FOR THE DECORATION

⅓ cup mini chocolate chips

Watermelon gummy candies

Black decorating icing, fitted with a small round tip (I like Wilton brand)

1. MAKE THE CUPCAKES: Preheat the oven to 350°F. Line two 12-cup cupcake tins with 15 liners.

2. In a medium bowl, whisk together the flour, cocoa powder, baking soda, and salt.

3. In a stand mixer fitted with the paddle attachment, beat the butter and sugar until light and fluffy, about 3 minutes. Beat in the eggs, one at a time, mixing after each addition. Beat in the sour cream, milk, vanilla, and enough food color to reach a deep red color until combined. Using a rubber spatula, fold in the dry ingredients. Divide the batter among the lined cupcake cups, filling them about two-thirds of the way.

4. Bake until a toothpick inserted into the center of the cupcakes comes out clean, 17 to 20 minutes. Let the cupcakes cool in the tins for 5 minutes. Then turn them out onto a wire rack and let them cool completely.

5. MAKE THE FROSTING: In a stand mixer fitted with the paddle attachment, beat the cream cheese and butter on medium speed until smooth. Add the confectioners' sugar gradually and beat until combined. Beat in the vanilla until combined. Scrape down the sides of the bowl. Beat the frosting on high speed until it is light and fluffy, about 2 minutes. Beat in enough green gel food color to reach a medium green. Transfer the frosting to a piping bag fitted with a large round tip.

6. DECORATE THE CUPCAKES: Pipe a dollop of the green frosting on top of each cupcake, and then sprinkle the mini chocolate chips on the frosting.

7. Pipe a kawaii face onto each watermelon gummy candy with the black decorating icing. Top each cupcake with a decorated gummy candy.

S'MORES CUPCAKES

MAKES
2 DOZEN
CUPCAKES

I have to admit, I've never been a fan of camping. The first (and last) time my family took me camping as a child, I became extremely stressed about whether my fruity shampoo would attract bears, or if the granola bar in my backpack would get eaten by a bear, or if our tent could protect us from bears at night. Basically I found out that my survival instinct may be too strong for roughing it outdoors. But the best part of camping? S'mores! These cupcakes have all the toasty, chocolatey flavor of s'mores, no campfire (or bear repellant) necessary.

FOR THE CRUST

1⅓ cups graham cracker crumbs (from 9 to 10 graham crackers)

2 tablespoons sugar

5 tablespoons unsalted butter, melted

FOR THE CUPCAKES

2 cups all-purpose flour

2 cups sugar

¾ cup natural unsweetened cocoa powder

2 teaspoons baking soda

1 teaspoon baking powder

1 teaspoon table salt

2 large eggs, at room temperature

1 cup buttermilk, at room temperature

½ cup canola oil

1 teaspoon vanilla extract

1 cup hot coffee

FOR THE DECORATIONS

3 cups mini marshmallows

6 graham crackers

24 large marshmallows

Black and pink edible ink markers (I like AmeriColor brand)

4 ounces chocolate candy coating, melted (about ¼ cup melted candy coating)

1. **MAKE THE CRUST:** Preheat the oven to 350°F. Line two 12-cup cupcake tins with liners.

2. In a medium bowl, stir together the graham cracker crumbs, sugar, and melted butter until combined. Scoop 1 tablespoon of the mixture onto the bottom of each cupcake liner and tamp it down with the end of rolling pin or a small glass.

3. Bake until the crusts are crisp, about 5 minutes. Let them cool in the tin for at least 10 minutes.

4. **MAKE THE CUPCAKES:** In a large bowl, whisk together the flour, sugar, cocoa powder, baking soda, baking powder, and salt. Add the eggs, buttermilk, oil, and vanilla. Using a handheld electric mixer, beat on medium speed until combined. Pour in the hot coffee and beat on medium speed until just combined. Pour the batter over the cooled crusts, filling the cups about three-fourths of the way.

5. Bake until a toothpick inserted into the center of the cupcakes comes out clean, 18 to 20 minutes. Let the cupcakes cool in the tins for 5 minutes. Then transfer them to a wire rack and let them cool completely.

6. **DECORATE THE CUPCAKES:** Preheat the oven to broil.

7. Place the cupcakes on a baking sheet. Cut the mini marshmallows in half, and arrange the halves, cut-side down, on top of each cupcake to cover the surface. Broil until the marshmallows are toasted, 15 to 20 seconds. Keep a close eye on them, as they can burn easily, and immediately remove the baking sheet from the broiler.

8. Using a serrated knife, cut each graham cracker into a 1¼ x 1-inch rectangle. (For a standard-size graham cracker, this means cutting the graham cracker into quarters, then cutting each quarter in half.)

9. Draw a face onto the side of each large marshmallow with the black and pink edible ink markers.

10. Dip the bottom of a large marshmallow into the melted chocolate candy coating and place it on top of a graham cracker square. Using a small spoon, dollop about ¼ teaspoon of the chocolate candy coating on top of each marshmallow and spread it so the chocolate is dripping down the sides. Top with another graham cracker square. Repeat with the remaining marshmallows. Let them set completely, about 10 minutes.

11. Using a dab of melted chocolate candy coating, place one graham-cracker-and-marshmallow topper on each cupcake.

ALPACA CUPCAKES

MAKES
2 DOZEN
CUPCAKES

While I have yet to meet a real-life alpaca, I can confirm by searching online for "baby alpaca" that these cute creatures are certifiably kawaii! It's no wonder that they recently seem to have risen in kawaii popularity, and they really are everywhere. I've seen alpaca plush, stationery, keychains—even onesies! With their fluffy fur of white nonpareils and bashful frosting eyes, these cupcakes mimic the best of the adorable animal.

FOR THE CUPCAKES

3 cups cake flour

2 cups sugar

2 teaspoons baking powder

½ teaspoon baking soda

1 teaspoon table salt

½ cup (1 stick) butter, cut into ½-inch
    cubes, at room temperature

4 large eggs, at room temperature

1 cup buttermilk, at room temperature

½ cup canola oil

4 teaspoons vanilla extract

FOR THE FROSTING

1 cup (2 sticks) unsalted butter,
    at room temperature

3 cups confectioners' sugar

1 teaspoon vanilla extract

2 tablespoons milk

FOR THE DECORATIONS

24 mini marshmallows

White nonpareils

24 white candy melts

Black decorating icing
    (I like Wilton brand)

Pink confetti quins

1. **MAKE THE CUPCAKES:** Preheat the oven to 350°F. Line two 12-cup cupcake tins with liners.

2. In a stand mixer fitted with the paddle attachment, combine the cake flour, sugar, baking powder, baking soda, and salt on low speed until well mixed, about 1 minute. With the mixer running on low speed, add the cubed butter and beat until the mixture resembles coarse sand, about 4 minutes. (For more on this technique, see page 23.)

3. In a separate bowl, whisk together the eggs, buttermilk, oil, and vanilla. With the mixer running on low speed, gradually add the wet ingredients to the dry ingredients and beat just until combined. Divide the batter among the lined cupcake cups, filling them about two-thirds of the way.

4. Bake until a toothpick inserted into the center of the cupcakes comes out clean, 16 to 18 minutes. Let the cupcakes cool in the tins for 5 minutes. Then turn them out onto a wire rack and let them cool completely.

5. **MAKE THE FROSTING:** In a stand mixer fitted with the paddle attachment, beat the butter on high speed until smooth, about 1 minute.

Reduce the speed to low, gradually add the confectioners' sugar, and beat until combined. Beat in the vanilla and milk until combined. Scrape down the sides of the bowl. Beat the frosting on medium-high speed until it is light and fluffy, about 3 minutes.

6. **DECORATE THE CUPCAKES:** Using an offset spatula, spread about 1½ tablespoons of the frosting on each cupcake and create a flat top. Clean off the spatula by scraping any excess frosting back into the frosting bowl, and then run the spatula at a 45-degree angle along the sides of each cupcake to create a flat edge.

7. Using kitchen scissors, cut the mini marshmallows in half diagonally. Place one half on each side of the cupcakes for ears. Sprinkle white nonpareils on the upper third of each cupcake for fur.

8. Place one white candy melt in the center of each cupcake for the base of the nose. Using the black decorating icing, pipe on the nose and eyes. Using tweezers, place one pink confetti quin next to each eye for cheeks.

CUPCAKE PIÑATA COOKIES

MAKES ABOUT 9 COOKIES

Cute piñatas stuffed with candy and treats are always crowd-pleasers. But I have very little hand-eye coordination. Pair that with a blindfold and a baseball bat, and you pretty much have a recipe for disaster. However, if there is one kind of piñata I am good at breaking open, it's one made of cookies. These surprise-filled cookies are a fun, colorful party treat with little risk of injury to boot!

FOR THE COOKIES

3 cups all-purpose flour

½ teaspoon baking powder

½ teaspoon table salt

1 cup (2 sticks) unsalted butter, at room temperature

1 cup sugar

1 large egg, at room temperature

2 teaspoons vanilla extract

FOR THE ICING

4 cups confectioners' sugar

3 tablespoons meringue powder

Black, pink, and purple gel food colors

FOR THE DECORATIONS

Jelly beans (or small candy of choice)

Rainbow sprinkles

Red candy-coated chocolates, such as M&Ms

1. MAKE THE COOKIES: In a large bowl, whisk together the flour, baking powder, and salt.

2. In a stand mixer fitted with the paddle attachment, combine the butter and sugar and beat on medium-high speed until light and fluffy, about 3 minutes. Add in the egg and vanilla and beat until combined. Scrape down the sides of the bowl. With the mixer running on low speed, gradually add the dry ingredients and beat until the dough comes together and no streaks of flour remain, about 1 minute. Divide the dough in half, form each half into a disk, and wrap each in plastic wrap. Refrigerate for at least 1 hour.

3. Preheat the oven to 350°F. Line a baking sheet with parchment paper.

4. On a floured work surface, use a rolling pin to roll out one disk of cookie dough until it is ¼ inch thick. Cut out cupcake-shaped cookies with a cupcake cookie cutter, and transfer the cookies to the prepared baking sheet. Gather the scraps and repeat

the rolling and cutting processes with the remaining disk of dough. Ensure that for each cupcake, you have three cutouts.

5. For one-third of the cookies, using a sharp knife, cut out the inner portion of the cookies, leaving a ½-inch border.

6. Bake all the cookies until the edges are a light golden brown, 10 to 12 minutes. Let them cool on the baking sheet for 5 minutes. Then transfer them to a wire rack to cool completely.

7. MAKE THE ICING: In a stand mixer fitted with the paddle attachment, combine the confectioners' sugar, meringue powder, and 5 tablespoons of water on high speed until smooth, about 7 minutes. If the icing is too thick, add water, 1 teaspoon at a time, and beat to combine. If you drag a knife through the icing, the line should disappear after 15 seconds.

8. Transfer 2 tablespoons of the icing to a separate bowl and color it black with the black gel food color. Transfer

(recipe continues)

COOKIES

the black icing to a small piping bag fitted with a small round tip or to a plastic zip-top bag and cut off a small tip.

9. Transfer ½ cup of the remaining icing to a separate bowl and color it pink with the pink gel food color.

10. Transfer ½ cup of the remaining icing to a separate bowl and color it purple with the purple gel food color. Leave the remaining icing white.

11. Place the pink, purple, and white icings in separate piping bags fitted with a small round tip or in plastic zip-top bags and cut off small tips.

12. Flip over a third of the whole cookies so the flat side is facing up. Pipe a border of white icing around the outside, and then place a cookie with the center cut out on top (see photo 1). Fill the center with jelly beans (see photo 2). Pipe more white icing around the outside border and place another whole cookie on top (see photo 3).

13. Frost the bottom part of half the cupcake cookies (the "wrappers") with the pink icing and the other half with the purple icing. Use the white icing to pipe the cupcake frosting on the top part of the cookie. Scatter the sprinkles over the white icing. Press a red candy-coated chocolate at the top of the cupcake for a cherry. Let the icing set for at least 30 minutes.

14. Pipe kawaii faces onto the cupcake wrappers with the black icing. Let the icing set until hardened, at least 6 hours.

GIANT PIZZA COOKIE

MAKES ONE 9-INCH COOKIE

There's a pizza place about ten minutes from my house that serves some of *the best* deep-dish Chicago-style pies. The crust is thick and crisp on the outside, there are juicy chunks of tomato in the sauce, and it's topped with the perfect amount of gooey cheese. It's a big, bold pizza that just hits the spot. This deep-dish cookie is in honor of those fantastic pies. I love this dessert because it's basically an extra-thick, soft, chewy, melt-in-your-mouth sugar cookie. Plus the decoration is beginner-friendly and you can customize it with your favorite candy "toppings." Dig in!

FOR THE COOKIE

Cooking spray

1 cup all-purpose flour

¾ teaspoon baking powder

¼ teaspoon table salt

½ cup (1 stick) unsalted butter, at room temperature

½ cup sugar

1 large egg, at room temperature

½ teaspoon vanilla extract

FOR THE FROSTING

½ cup (1 stick) unsalted butter, at room temperature

1½ cups confectioners' sugar

½ teaspoon vanilla extract

4½ teaspoons milk

Red gel food color

1. MAKE THE COOKIE: Preheat the oven to 350°F. Lightly grease a 9-inch springform pan with cooking spray.

2. In a large bowl, whisk together the flour, baking powder, and salt.

3. In a stand mixer fitted with the paddle attachment, combine the butter and sugar and beat until light and fluffy, about 3 minutes. Add in the egg and vanilla and beat until combined. Scrape down the sides of the bowl. With the mixer on low speed, gradually add in the dry ingredients and beat until combined. Press the cookie dough into the prepared pan.

4. Bake until the edges of the cookie are golden brown, 20 to 22 minutes. Let the cookie cool in the pan for 5 minutes. Then remove the sides of the springform pan and transfer the cookie to a wire rack to cool completely. Once it has cooled, lift the cookie off the bottom of the springform pan.

5. MAKE THE FROSTING: In a stand mixer fitted with the paddle attachment, beat the butter on high speed until smooth, about 1 minute. Reduce the speed to low, gradually add the confectioners' sugar, and beat until combined. Add in the vanilla and milk and beat until combined. Scrape down the sides of the bowl. Beat the frosting on medium-high speed until it is light and fluffy, about 3 minutes.

6. Transfer 1 tablespoon of the frosting to a piping bag fitted with a small tip.

7. Dye the remaining frosting red with the red gel food color.

(recipe and ingredients continue)

1 cup sweetened flaked coconut

Strawberry fruit leather candy

3 green gummy fish

2 chocolate candy melts

1 teaspoon melted chocolate chips

2 tablespoons chocolate-covered raisins

2 pink jelly beans

8. DECORATE THE COOKIE:
Preheat the oven to 325°F. Line a small baking sheet with parchment paper.

9. Spread the flaked coconut evenly over the prepared baking sheet and toast it until it is golden brown, 5 to 10 minutes. Keep a close eye on it to make sure it does not burn. Let the coconut cool completely.

10. Cut out rounds of the fruit leather candy with a 1-inch round cookie cutter to make the "pepperoni slices."

11. Cut the green gummy fish into ⅛-inch pieces to make the "green bell peppers."

12. Pipe a small amount of the white frosting in the upper corner of the chocolate candy melts for the pupils.

13. Spread the red frosting evenly over the cookie, leaving a ½-inch border for the crust. Sprinkle the toasted coconut on top, and then place the eyes on the lower third of the cookie. Pipe on the mouth with the melted chocolate. Place a pink jelly bean beside each eye for cheeks.

14. Arrange the toppings—the fruit leather rounds, green gummy fish, and chocolate-covered raisins (for sausage)—on the pizza as desired.

If the icing is too thick to spoon over the cookies, simply add more water, 1/2 teaspoon at a time, until it's thin enough to drip easily over the sides of the cookies.

ICED ANIMAL COOKIES

**MAKES ABOUT
5 DOZEN
COOKIES**

During my freshman fall quarter at Stanford, it was tradition that my computer science programming partner and I would celebrate finishing a project by chowing down on these classic cookies. At least, that had been the idea at the beginning of the year. By the end of the quarter, we'd be stuck fixing a bug at 1:34 a.m. when one of us would weakly mutter, "Can we eat some of the cookies?" At which point we'd cross our fingers that the distraction and burst of sugar would magically fix our program. While I can't promise these colorful cookies will write code for you, I *can* promise that they'll bring a smile to your face as soon as you bite into one.

FOR THE COOKIES

1½ cups all-purpose flour

¼ teaspoon baking powder

¼ teaspoon table salt

½ cup (1 stick) unsalted butter, at room temperature

½ cup sugar

1 large egg, at room temperature

1 teaspoon vanilla extract

FOR THE ICING

6 cups confectioners' sugar

6 tablespoons light corn syrup

Pink gel food color

FOR THE DECORATIONS

Rainbow nonpareil sprinkles

1. **MAKE THE COOKIES:** In a large bowl, whisk together the flour, baking powder, and salt.

2. In a stand mixer fitted with the paddle attachment, combine the butter and sugar and beat on medium-high speed until light and fluffy, about 3 minutes. Scrape down the sides of the bowl. Add in the egg and vanilla and beat until combined. Scrape down the sides of the bowl once again. With the mixer running on low speed, gradually add the dry ingredients to the wet ingredients. Beat until the dough comes together and no streaks of flour remain, about 1 minute. Wrap the dough in plastic wrap and refrigerate it for at least 1 hour.

3. Preheat the oven to 350°F. Line two baking sheets with parchment paper.

4. On a floured work surface, use a rolling pin to roll out the cookie dough until it is ¼ inch thick. Using animal cookie cutters that are about 1½ inches in diameter, cut out animal shapes. Transfer the cookies to the prepared baking sheets, spacing them 1 inch apart. Gather the scraps and repeat the rolling and cutting processes with the remaining dough.

5. Bake the cookies until the edges are a light golden brown, 8 to 10 minutes. Let them cool on the baking sheet for 5 minutes. Then transfer them to a wire rack to cool completely.

6. **MAKE THE ICING:** In a large bowl, whisk together the confectioners' sugar, light corn syrup, and 6 tablespoons of water until smooth. Transfer half of the icing to a separate bowl and dye it pink with the gel food color.

7. **DECORATE THE COOKIES:** Place a sheet of parchment paper under the wire rack to catch any icing drips. Spoon the pink icing over half of the cooled cookies to coat them (see note on opposite page), and then tap the wire rack on the counter to distribute the icing evenly. If necessary, scrape the excess icing off the parchment paper with a spatula and use it to coat the remaining cookies that get pink icing. Decorate those cookies with rainbow sprinkles. Repeat for the other half of the cookies, using the white icing and more sprinkles.

8. Let the icing set for at least 1 hour.

OATMEAL BEAR COOKIES

MAKES 2 DOZEN COOKIES

Okay, let's get things straight about these oatmeal cookies. *These oatmeal cookies are not boring.* They're not the cookies you leave behind on the holiday cookie platter in favor of chocolate chip, peanut butter, or any other treat for that matter. They're buttery, chewy, crispy-on-the-outside deliciousness. And because their bumpy texture reminds me of a fluffy stuffed bear toy I adored as a child, I decided to decorate them to look as enticing as they taste. With a charming raisin nose and chocolate chip eyes, they're absolutely irresistible and far from boring. Can you imagine one of these fresh from the oven with a tall glass of milk? Heaven! Trust me, you need these in your life.

2 cups all-purpose flour

1 teaspoon baking soda

1½ teaspoons ground cinnamon

1 teaspoon table salt

1 cup (2 sticks) unsalted butter, at room temperature

1 cup granulated sugar

1 cup (packed) light brown sugar

2 large eggs, at room temperature

1 teaspoon vanilla extract

3 cups quick-cooking oats

⅓ cup raisins, chopped, plus 24 whole raisins

⅓ cup mini chocolate chips

⅓ cup roasted salted pecans, finely chopped

48 chocolate chips

1. Preheat the oven to 350°F. Line two baking sheets with parchment paper.

2. In a large bowl, whisk together the flour, baking soda, cinnamon, and salt.

3. In a stand mixer fitted with the paddle attachment, combine the butter, granulated sugar, and brown sugar and beat until light and fluffy, about 3 minutes. Add in the eggs, one at a time, mixing after each addition. Add in the vanilla and beat until combined. Scrape down the sides of the bowl. With the mixer running on low speed, gradually add the dry ingredients and beat until a dough forms. Add the oats, chopped raisins, mini chocolate chips, and chopped pecans, and beat until just combined.

4. Scoop 2-tablespoon-size balls of dough (the size of a Ping-Pong ball) about 3 inches apart on the prepared baking sheets. For the best results, ensure that a side of the cookie with few visible mix-ins is face up on the baking sheet. Flatten each cookie slightly. On each side of a cookie, place ½-teaspoon-size balls of dough (the size of a marble) for ears. Be sure to leave about ¼ inch of space between the ear and the cookie because the cookies will spread. Place a raisin on each cookie for a nose, and press the point of a chocolate chip into the cookie on either side of the nose for eyes. Note that the face will spread out in the oven, so place the eyes right beside the nose and be sure to press them into the cookie so the surface is flush.

5. Bake until the edges begin to turn golden brown, 13 to 15 minutes. Let the cookies cool on the baking sheet for 5 minutes. Then transfer them to a wire rack to cool completely.

PEANUT BUTTER LION COOKIES

MAKES ABOUT 40 COOKIES

It's no secret in my family that I *love* peanut butter. Smooth, crunchy, low-sodium, high-sodium—I'm happy as long there's a jar around. And in my opinion, the only thing better than peanut butter on a spoon is peanut butter in a cookie! This recipe is my tried-and-true, absolute favorite for peanut butter cookies. And because the golden color reminded me of fluffy lion fur, I decided to pipe manes of melted chocolate to transform them into ferociously cute felines!

FOR THE COOKIES

2½ cups all-purpose flour

1 teaspoon table salt

½ teaspoon baking soda

½ teaspoon baking powder

1 cup (2 sticks) unsalted butter, at room temperature

1 cup (packed) light brown sugar

1 cup granulated sugar

1 cup creamy peanut butter (not natural; see note on opposite page)

2 large eggs, at room temperature

2 teaspoons vanilla extract

FOR THE DECORATIONS

120 chocolate chips

1½ cups semisweet chocolate chips, melted

1 tablespoon white chocolate chips, melted

1. MAKE THE COOKIES: Preheat the oven to 350°F. Line two baking sheets with parchment paper.

2. In a large bowl, whisk together the flour, salt, baking soda, and baking powder.

3. In a stand mixer fitted with the paddle attachment, combine the butter, light brown sugar, and granulated sugar and beat on medium-high speed until light and fluffy, about 3 minutes. Add in the peanut butter and beat until combined. Add in the eggs, one at a time, mixing after each addition. Add in the vanilla and beat until combined. Scrape down the sides of the bowl. With the mixer running on low speed, gradually add the dry ingredients and beat until a dough just comes together. Scrape down the sides of the bowl as necessary.

4. Scoop 2-tablespoon-size dough balls (the size of a Ping-Pong ball) onto the prepared baking sheets, leaving about 2 inches between them. Flatten each ball slightly.

5. Bake until the edges begin to turn golden brown, 10 to 12 minutes. Let the cookies cool on the baking sheets for 2 minutes. Then, working quickly while the cookies are still warm, press the side of one chocolate chip with the point facing down into each cookie for a nose. Press the points of two chocolate chips into each cookie for eyes. (Press in the nose before the eyes to help center the face.) Let the cookies cool for 5 more minutes. Then transfer them to a wire rack to cool completely.

6. DECORATE THE COOKIES: Place the melted semisweet chocolate chips in a plastic zip-top bag and cut off a small tip. Pipe on the lion's mouth and mane.

7. Place the melted white chocolate in a plastic zip-top bag and cut off a small tip. Pipe a small amount of melted white chocolate in the upper corner of the lion's eyes and let the decoration set completely, about 10 minutes.

Natural peanut butter has a different consistency and composition that is less suitable for baking.

CHOCOLATE MONKEY COOKIES

MAKES ABOUT 32 COOKIES

These aren't just chocolate cookies. These are ooey-gooey, rich, deep, dark chocolate cookies. And best of all, the deep color makes them the perfect choice for a monkey shape! At least, that's what I see when I look at them. Just add the signature ears, a crunchy vanilla wafer mouth, and some chocolate details. You'll have a treat that your friends will go bananas for!

FOR THE COOKIES

2 cups all-purpose flour

¾ cup natural unsweetened cocoa powder

1 teaspoon baking soda

½ teaspoon table salt

1 cup (2 sticks) unsalted butter, at room temperature

⅔ cup granulated sugar

⅔ cup (packed) light brown sugar

2 large eggs, at room temperature

1 teaspoon vanilla extract

1½ cups dark chocolate chips

FOR THE DECORATIONS

¼ cup semisweet chocolate chips, melted

32 vanilla wafer cookies

64 white chocolate chips

1. In a large bowl, whisk together the flour, cocoa powder, baking soda, and salt.

2. In a stand mixer fitted with the paddle attachment, combine the butter, granulated sugar, and brown sugar and beat until light and fluffy, about 3 minutes. Add in the eggs, one at a time, mixing after each addition. Add in the vanilla and beat until combined. Scrape down the sides of the bowl. With the mixer running on low speed, gradually add the dry ingredients and beat until a dough forms, about 1 minute. Add the chocolate chips and beat to combine. Cover the dough with plastic wrap and refrigerate for at least 30 minutes.

3. Preheat the oven to 350°F. Line two baking sheets with parchment paper.

4. Scoop 2-tablespoon-size balls of dough (the size of a Ping-Pong ball) about 3 inches apart onto the prepared baking sheets. On each side of a cookie, place ½-teaspoon-size balls of dough (the size of a marble) for ears. Be sure to leave about ¼ inch of space between the ear and the cookie because the cookies will spread.

5. Bake until the cookies are just set, 10 to 12 minutes. Let them cool on the baking sheets for 5 minutes. Then transfer them to a wire rack to cool completely.

6. DECORATE THE COOKIES: Place the melted semisweet chocolate in a plastic zip-top bag with a small corner cut off. Pipe a small amount of the melted chocolate onto the back of a vanilla wafer cookie and press it onto a chocolate cookie. Pipe a dot of melted chocolate on each side of the vanilla cookie and then press the point of a white chocolate chip into the melted chocolate to make the eyes. Pipe on the pupils and a smile with the melted chocolate. Repeat for each cookie.

KAWAII ROYAL ICING COOKIES

MAKES ABOUT 40 COOKIES

Some things are just better together: milk and cookies, eggs and bacon, peanut butter and jelly, and the list goes on! These cookies highlight some of my favorite combos as cute kawaii pairs. I just love how you can use royal icing to turn a blank canvas of a cookie into a work of kawaii art. These classic cookies are perfect for playing and experimenting with, so feel free to try out some of your own favorite pairings.

FOR THE COOKIES

3 cups all-purpose flour

½ teaspoon baking powder

½ teaspoon table salt

1 cup (2 sticks) unsalted butter, at room temperature

1 cup sugar

1 large egg, at room temperature

2 teaspoons vanilla extract

FOR THE ROYAL ICING

8 cups plus ½ teaspoon confectioners' sugar

6 tablespoons meringue powder

Black, brown, blue, purple, yellow, and red gel food colors

FOR THE DECORATIONS

1¼ teaspoons mini chocolate chips

1. **MAKE THE COOKIES:** In a large bowl, whisk together the flour, baking powder, and salt.

2. In a stand mixer fitted with the paddle attachment, combine the butter and sugar and beat on medium-high speed until light and fluffy, about 3 minutes. Scrape down the sides of the bowl. Add in the egg and vanilla and beat until combined. With the mixer running on low speed, gradually add the dry ingredients to the wet ingredients. Beat until a dough comes together and no streaks of flour remain, about 1 minute. Divide the dough in half, form each half into a disk, and wrap each in plastic wrap. Refrigerate for at least 1 hour.

3. Preheat the oven to 350°F. Line two baking sheets with parchment paper.

4. On a floured work surface, use a rolling pin to roll out one disk of cookie dough until it is ¼ inch thick. Using a sharp knife (see note, opposite), cut out the cookies according to the templates (see page 231). Transfer the cookies to the prepared baking sheets. Gather the scraps and repeat the rolling and cutting processes with the remaining disk of dough.

5. Bake the cookies until the edges are a light golden brown, 12 to 13 minutes. Let them cool on the baking sheets for 5 minutes. Then transfer them to a wire rack to cool completely.

6. **MAKE THE ICING:** In a stand mixer fitted with the paddle attachment, combine the 8 cups of confectioners' sugar with the meringue powder and ½ cup plus 2 tablespoons of water. Blend on high speed until smooth, about 7 minutes. If the icing is too thick, add water, 1 teaspoon at a time, and beat to combine. If you drag a knife through the icing, the line should disappear after 15 seconds.

(recipe continues)

When cutting out the cookies, avoid dragging the knife along the entire perimeter of the template. Instead, gently wiggle the knife up and down as you go around the outside to avoid pulling and distorting the shape of the cookie.

7. Divide and color the icing as follows (you will have some leftover white icing in case you need to adjust or lighten colors):

> 6 tablespoons white icing
>
> 1½ teaspoons yellow icing
>
> 2 tablespoons pink icing
>
> 5 tablespoons red icing
>
> 3 tablespoons dark brown icing
>
> 2 tablespoons purple icing
>
> 5 tablespoons tan icing
>
> 4 tablespoons light tan icing
>
> 3 tablespoons blue icing
>
> 2 tablespoons black icing

8. Add the remaining ½ teaspoon confectioners' sugar to the black icing to thicken it. Transfer all of the icing to piping bags fitted with small round tips or to plastic zip-top bags and cut off small tips.

9. **DECORATE THE COOKIES: FOR THE CHOCOLATE CHIP COOKIE:** Pipe a border around the outside of the cookie using the tan icing. Fill in the outline with more tan icing and spread it evenly with a toothpick. Sprinkle about ¼ teaspoon mini chocolate chips on each cookie, leaving the bottom third of the cookie open for a face. Let set for about 30 minutes. Pipe on kawaii faces using the black and pink icings.

10. **FOR THE MILK BOTTLE:** Pipe a rectangle border of blue icing in the middle of the bottle to make a label. Pipe on the cap using the red icing. Let the icing set for about 30 minutes.

Then pipe on kawaii faces and the milk label using the black and pink icings. Pipe a border of white icing around the remaining portion of the bottle above and below the label and fill it in with more white icing. Spread the icing evenly with a toothpick.

11. **FOR THE PEANUT BUTTER AND JELLY TOAST:** Pipe a border around the outside of the toast using the dark brown icing. In the center, pipe a blob of either tan icing for peanut butter or purple icing for jelly. Let the icing set for about 30 minutes. Pipe on kawaii faces using the black and pink icings. Fill in the toast with the light tan icing.

12. **FOR THE BACON:** Pipe a border of red icing around the outside of the cookie, then fill it in with more red icing. Pipe lines of pink icing over the red icing to make the bacon fat. Let the icing set for about 30 minutes. Pipe on kawaii faces using the black and pink icings.

13. **FOR THE EGG:** Pipe on a circle of yellow icing in the center of the cookies. Pipe a border of white icing around the egg yolk and around the outside of the cookie. Fill in the space with more white icing and spread it evenly with a toothpick. Let the icing set for about 30 minutes. Pipe on kawaii faces using black and pink icings.

14. Let all the cookies set until the icing has completely hardened, at least 6 hours.

LEMON EMOJI COOKIES

MAKES ABOUT 15 COOKIES

I use too many emojis. I can't help it. I love how they add that extra bit of personality and enthusiasm to a text. So if you ever receive a text message from me, don't be alarmed by the emoji-to-text ratio! I funnel my love of emojis into these puffy lemon cookies and decorate them with my favorite expressions, but feel free to get creative and use your own top picks to adorn your creations.

FOR THE COOKIES

2 cups all-purpose flour

2 teaspoons baking powder

½ teaspoon table salt

½ cup (1 stick) unsalted butter, at room temperature

1 cup granulated sugar

1 tablespoon grated lemon zest

1 large egg, at room temperature

2 tablespoons fresh lemon juice

½ teaspoon vanilla extract

½ cup confectioners' sugar

Yellow gel food color

FOR THE ICING

2 cups confectioners' sugar

4½ teaspoons meringue powder

Blue and black gel food color

FOR THE DECORATIONS

Large red heart sprinkles

1. MAKE THE COOKIES: Preheat the oven to 350°F. Line two baking sheets with parchment paper.

2. In a large bowl, whisk together the flour, baking powder, and salt.

3. In a stand mixer fitted with the paddle attachment, combine the butter and granulated sugar and beat on medium-high speed until light and fluffy, about 3 minutes. Add in the lemon zest, then the egg, and beat until combined. Add in the lemon juice and vanilla and beat until combined. With the mixer running on low speed, gradually add the dry ingredients and beat until the dough just comes together, about 1 minute.

4. Place the confectioners' sugar in a shallow dish. Scoop out 2-tablespoon-size balls of dough (the size of a Ping-Pong ball), roll them in the confectioners' sugar, and place them about 3 inches apart on the prepared baking sheets. Flatten each ball slightly.

5. Bake until the edges are set and a light golden brown, 10 to 12 minutes (see note on page 111). Let the cookies cool on the baking sheets for about 5 minutes. Then transfer them to a wire rack to cool completely.

6. MAKE THE ICING: In a stand mixer fitted with the paddle attachment, combine the confectioners' sugar, meringue powder, and 5 tablespoons of water on high speed until smooth, about 7 minutes. If the icing is too thick, add water 1 teaspoon at a time, and beat to combine. If you drag a knife through the icing, the line should disappear after 15 seconds.

7. Transfer 3 tablespoons of the icing to a separate bowl and color it light blue with the blue gel food color. Transfer it to a small piping bag fitted with a small round tip.

8. Transfer 2 tablespoons of the remaining white icing to a small piping bag fitted with a small round tip.

9. Dye the remaining icing black with the black gel food color and transfer it to a piping bag fitted with a small round tip.

10. Pipe out kawaii emoji faces on the cookies using all of the colored icing (see photo on the following page for ideas). Use the large red heart sprinkles for eyes on the heart eye cookies. Let the icing set until hardened, at least 6 hours.

To ensure that these cookies remain soft and chewy on the inside, remove them from the oven as soon as the edges turn golden brown. The centers may seem soft if you poke them, but they will set up as they continue to cool on the baking sheets.

It may seem that 20 to 40 minutes is a large time range for letting the macarons rest, but it's so broad because the length of time will largely depend on the humidity of your climate. Start checking them at 20 minutes; then continue to check them at 5-minute intervals after that.

CLOUD MACARONS

That's right—we're making macarons, and there's no reason to be scared! I know these French cookies are intimidating to many home cooks, but I promise that with these instructions, you'll be churning them out like a Parisian pâtisserie. All it takes is patience and practice. I gave these macarons a cloud form because the shape is simple to create. Tuck in a bit of candy for decoration, and voilà! A delicious French treat with a kawaii twist.

FOR THE MACARONS

1¾ cups confectioners' sugar

1 cup finely ground almond flour

3 large egg whites, at room temperature

¼ teaspoon cream of tartar

¼ cup granulated sugar

FOR THE FROSTING

1 cup (2 sticks) unsalted butter, at room temperature

3 cups confectioners' sugar

1 teaspoon vanilla extract

2 tablespoons milk

Decorating icing in black and pink, fitted with small round tips (I like Wilton brand)

FOR THE DECORATIONS

Rainbow sour candy belts, such as Airhead Xtremes, cut into 1-inch pieces

Blue sour candy strips, such as Sour Punch Straws, cut into thin 1-inch pieces

Black and pink decorating icing (I like Wilton brand)

1. MAKE THE MACARONS: Line two baking sheets with parchment paper.

2. In a medium bowl, sift together the confectioners' sugar and almond flour.

3. In a large bowl, using a handheld electric mixer, combine the egg whites and cream of tartar and beat on high speed until foamy, about 30 seconds. Reduce the speed to medium and gradually add the granulated sugar. Increase the speed to high and beat until stiff, glossy peaks form, 7 to 8 minutes. Using a rubber spatula, fold half of the dry ingredients into the meringue mixture. Then add the remaining dry ingredients and continue folding until the batter runs off the spatula slowly but continuously.

4. Transfer the batter to a piping bag and pipe out cloud shapes that are about 2 inches wide onto the prepared baking sheets. Tap the baking sheets gently on the counter to release any air bubbles, and then let the macarons rest until a skin forms on top, 20 to 40 minutes (see note on opposite page). The rested macarons should not stick to your finger when lightly tapped.

5. Meanwhile, preheat the oven to 300°F.

6. Bake the macarons until the edges just begin to turn golden brown, 12 to 15 minutes. Let them cool completely on the baking sheets.

7. MAKE THE FROSTING: In a stand mixer fitted with the paddle attachment, beat the butter on high speed until smooth, about 1 minute. Reduce the speed to low, gradually add the confectioners' sugar, and beat until combined. Add in the vanilla and milk and beat until combined. Scrape down the sides of the bowl. Beat the frosting on medium-high speed until it is light and fluffy, about 3 minutes. Transfer the frosting to a piping bag or a large zip-top plastic bag.

8. DECORATE THE MERINGUES: Flip half of the macarons over and pipe frosting on the flat surfaces.

9. Place the cut sections of rainbow and blue sour candy on the frosting so they peek out over the sides and bottom of the macaron, respectively, then sandwich another macaron on top.

10. Using the black and pink decorating icing, pipe on kawaii faces.

FALL LEAF COOKIES

MAKES
ABOUT
24 COOKIES

If there's one high-school exam I'll never forget, it's the infamous "tree test." In our environmental science class, we had to learn how to identify more than twenty types of trees just by looking at the leaves. So, I can confidently tell you that these cookies are the simple, palmate lobed leaves of the *Acer macrophyllum,* or bigleaf maple. I dedicate these cookies to you, Mr. Willats—thank you for enhancing my science and cookie-baking capabilities!

FOR THE COOKIES

3½ cups all-purpose flour

½ teaspoon baking powder

½ teaspoon table salt

1 cup (2 sticks) unsalted butter,
at room temperature

½ cup granulated sugar

½ cup (packed) light brown sugar

1 large egg, at room temperature

1 cup pure Grade A maple syrup

2 teaspoons vanilla extract

Red, orange, yellow, and brown
gel food colors

FOR THE DECORATIONS

¼ cup chocolate chips, melted

1. **MAKE THE COOKIES:** In a large bowl, whisk together the flour, baking powder, and salt.

2. In a stand mixer fitted with the paddle attachment, combine the butter, granulated sugar, and brown sugar and beat on medium-high speed until light and fluffy, about 3 minutes. Add in the egg, ½ cup of the maple syrup, and the vanilla and beat until combined. Scrape down the sides of the bowl. With the mixer running on low speed, gradually add the dry ingredients. Beat until the dough comes together and no streaks of flour remain, about 1 minute.

3. Turn the dough out onto a floured work surface and divide it into quarters. Color one quarter of the dough yellow with the red gel food color, then transfer the dough to a piece of plastic wrap, form it into a disk, and wrap it tightly. Repeat for the remaining portions of dough using the orange, yellow, and brown gel food colors. Refrigerate all the disks for at least 30 minutes.

4. Preheat the oven to 350°F. Line two baking sheets with parchment paper.

5. On a floured work surface, divide each quarter of colored dough into thirds, and using your hands, roll each third into an 8-inch-long log. Place the logs next to one another so the colors alternate red, orange, yellow, and brown. Twist the colors together to make three thick logs, each composed of four colors. Roll each log into a ball so that the colors are marbled. Reserve one ball of dough, then wrap the remaining dough in plastic wrap and refrigerate them.

6. Roll out the reserved dough ball onto a floured work surface with a rolling pin until it is ¼ inch thick. Cut out leaf cookies with a leaf cookie cutter. Transfer the cookies to the prepared baking sheets, spacing them 1½ inches apart. Gather the scraps and repeat the rolling and cutting processes with the remaining balls of dough, working with one ball at a time.

7. Bake the cookies until the edges are a light golden brown, 10 to 12 minutes. Let them cool on the baking sheets for 5 minutes. Then use a pastry brush to brush the cookies with the remaining ½ cup of maple syrup. Transfer the cookies to a wire rack to cool completely. After about 20 minutes, the cookies will still be shiny but the syrup will no longer be tacky.

8. **DECORATE THE COOKIES:** Place the melted chocolate into a small plastic zip-top bag and cut off a small tip. Pipe on kawaii faces.

OWL SNICKERDOODLES

MAKES
ABOUT
30 COOKIES

This snickerdoodle recipe is another Fong family classic. It's in a book that's covered with cinnamon-butter fingerprints, scribbled with annotations, and dotted with a few crumbs in the spine. While I love the recipe as is, I thought these cinnamon-speckled cookies would be the perfect base for some adorable owls. Their light beige color ensures that the chocolate wings and bright yellow beak pop, making for a "hoot" of a cute cookie!

FOR THE COOKIES

1¾ cups sugar

1 tablespoon plus 1 teaspoon ground cinnamon

2¾ cups all-purpose flour

2 teaspoons baking powder

½ teaspoon table salt

1 cup (2 sticks) unsalted butter, at room temperature

2 large eggs, at room temperature

½ teaspoon vanilla extract

FOR THE DECORATIONS

30 large marshmallows

⅔ cup chocolate chips, melted

60 brown candy-coated chocolates, such as M&M's

30 yellow candy-coated chocolates, such as M&M's

1. MAKE THE COOKIES: Preheat the oven to 350°F. Line two baking sheets with parchment paper.

2. In a shallow dish, whisk together ¼ cup of the sugar and 1 tablespoon of the cinnamon. Set aside.

3. In a large bowl, whisk together the flour, baking powder, salt, and remaining 1 teaspoon cinnamon.

4. In a stand mixer fitted with the paddle attachment, combine the butter and remaining 1½ cups sugar and beat on medium-high speed until light and fluffy, about 3 minutes. Add in the eggs, one at a time, mixing after each addition. Add in the vanilla and beat until combined. Scrape down the sides of the bowl. With the mixer running on low speed, gradually add the flour mixture and beat until just combined.

5. Scoop out 2-tablespoon-size balls of dough (the size of a Ping-Pong ball) and roll them in the cinnamon-sugar mixture. Place the balls on the prepared baking sheets, leaving about 3 inches between cookies. Flatten the balls slightly.

6. Bake until the edges of the cookies are a light golden brown, about 11 minutes. Let them cool on the baking sheet for 5 minutes. Then transfer them to a wire rack and let them cool completely.

7. DECORATE THE COOKIES: Cut the marshmallows in half crosswise.

8. Place the melted chocolate in a small plastic zip-top bag and cut off a small corner. Pipe a small amount of chocolate on the cut side of each marshmallow and place two halves in the center of each cookie, sticky-side facing down, as part of the eyes.

9. Place a brown candy-covered chocolate on the inner part of each marshmallow for the pupils, using melted chocolate as "glue." Pipe chocolate on one side of each yellow chocolate-covered candy and place them between the marshmallows for a beak.

10. Pipe chocolate on the sides of the cookies for wings, then pipe V's under the eyes for feathers. Let the chocolate set completely, about 10 minutes.

PIES & PASTRIES

If the icing is too runny to pipe, simply mix in more confectioners' sugar! It should be slightly thicker than liquid glue.

KAWAII CUT-OUT APPLE PIE

MAKES
ONE 9-INCH
PIE

They say an apple a day keeps the doctor away, so if you have, like, half of this pie, you should be good for at least a month, right? That's my favorite kind of math. This classic treat comes with a kawaii twist: a top crust composed of adorable bunnies, hearts, and a flower to finish it off. Serve a slice of it warm with a scoop of ice cream, then grab a blanket, put on your favorite TV show, and tell the doctor you are taking good care of yourself!

FOR THE PIE

6 medium baking apples, such as Golden Delicious, Honeycrisp, or Gala

½ cup granulated sugar

½ cup (packed) light brown sugar

2 tablespoons cornstarch

2 tablespoons all-purpose flour

1 teaspoon ground cinnamon

¼ teaspoon ground ginger

¼ teaspoon ground nutmeg

1 tablespoon fresh lemon juice

2 disks Pie Crust Dough, homemade (page 122) or store-bought

1 large egg, at room temperature

1 tablespoon milk

3 tablespoons white sanding sugar

FOR THE ICING

1 cup confectioners' sugar

1. **MAKE THE PIE:** Preheat the oven to 375°F.

2. Peel, core, and cut the apples into ¼-inch-thick slices.

3. In a large bowl, whisk together the granulated sugar, brown sugar, cornstarch, flour, cinnamon, ginger, and nutmeg. Using a rubber spatula, fold in the apples. Add the lemon juice and fold again.

4. On a floured work surface, using a rolling pin, roll out one disk of the pie crust dough into a 13-inch round. Place it in a 9-inch pie plate and crimp the edges by pinching the crust between your thumb and forefinger. Pour the apple mixture into the crust.

5. Roll out the remaining disk of pie crust dough until it is ¼ inch thick. Cut out your desired kawaii shapes (bears, bunnies, hearts, etc.). Arrange the shapes on top of the pie in concentric circles.

6. In a small bowl, whisk together the egg and milk. Using a pastry brush, brush the mixture over the top of the pie. Sprinkle the white sanding sugar over the top of the pie.

7. Bake the pie for 20 minutes. Then cover the edges of the pie crust with foil to prevent over-browning and continue baking until the crust is a deep golden brown, about 25 minutes. Let the pie cool for at least 15 minutes before decorating it.

8. **MAKE THE ICING:** In a medium bowl, whisk the confectioners' sugar with 1 tablespoon of water until smooth. Transfer the icing to a piping bag fitted with a small round tip.

9. **DECORATE THE PIE:** Pipe the icing on top of the cooled pie as desired for white accents.

PIE CRUST DOUGH

**MAKES TWO
9-INCH
PIE CRUSTS**

When it comes to pies, I like a flaky, buttery, melt-in-your-mouth, crisp crust. This recipe is my absolute favorite, and you'll find that it's used in many of the recipes in this chapter. If you're like me and get too impatient to cut butter into flour by hand, using a food processor is an easy fix. I've provided instructions for both techniques here. This crust comes together in minutes and it's a hundred times flakier than store-bought, though the latter will do in a pinch.

2½ cups all-purpose flour

1 tablespoon sugar

½ teaspoon table salt

1 cup (2 sticks) unsalted butter, cold, cut into ½-inch cubes

BY HAND: In a large bowl, whisk together the flour, sugar, and salt. Using a pastry cutter or two knives, cut in the butter until the mixture resembles fine crumbs. Stir in 6 to 7 tablespoons of cold water, 1 tablespoon at a time, until the dough forms a ball.

WITH A FOOD PROCESSOR: In a food processor, combine the flour, sugar, and salt and process until fully mixed, about 30 seconds. Add the cubed butter and pulse until the mixture resembles fine crumbs. Add 6 to 7 tablespoons of cold water, 1 tablespoon at a time, pulsing until the mixture comes together when pressed in your hands.

Divide the dough in half and shape each half into a disk. Wrap the disks in plastic wrap and refrigerate for at least 30 minutes before using.

If you are making the dough in advance, place the wrapped disks in a sealable freezer bag and label it with the date. The dough will keep in the refrigerator for up to 3 days, or in the freezer for up to 3 months.

PEANUT BUTTER PUG PIE

MAKES ONE 9-INCH PIE

This peanut butter pie is one of my favorite recipes, and it happens to be the perfect color to transform into an adorable pug. All it takes is just a few chocolate decorations and bits of candy! This dessert has a crunchy, buttery chocolate cookie crust and a smooth, creamy peanut butter filling that will make you want to wag your tail with joy.

FOR THE CRUST

25 chocolate sandwich cookies, such as Oreos

¼ cup (½ stick) unsalted butter, melted

FOR THE FILLING

1½ cups heavy whipping cream, cold

8 ounces cream cheese, at room temperature

1 cup creamy peanut butter (not natural; see note on page 103)

½ cup confectioners' sugar

FOR THE DECORATIONS

4 ounces chocolate candy coating, melted (about ¼ cup melted candy coating)

2 chocolate candy melts

1 teaspoon melted white candy coating

1 teaspoon melted pink candy coating

1 brown candy-coated peanut chocolate, such as a peanut M&M

1. MAKE THE CRUST: In a food processor, pulse the chocolate sandwich cookies into fine crumbs. Add the melted butter and pulse to combine. Pour the crust mixture into a 9-inch pie plate and press it over the bottom and up the sides. Refrigerate the crust while you make the filling.

2. MAKE THE FILLING: In a large bowl, using a handheld electric mixer, beat the heavy whipping cream on high speed until stiff peaks form, about 3 minutes.

3. In a stand mixer fitted with the paddle attachment, combine the cream cheese, peanut butter, and confectioners' sugar and beat on medium-high speed until smooth, about 2 minutes. Fold in the whipped cream. Spoon the mixture into the crust and smooth the top with an offset spatula. Refrigerate the pie while you make the decorations.

4. DECORATE THE PIE: To make the ears, muzzle, and tongue, place a sheet of parchment paper over the template (see page 233). Spoon the melted chocolate and pink candy coating onto the parchment and spread them out according to the template. Let the coating set completely at room temperature, about 10 minutes.

5. To make the eyes, dab a small amount of melted white candy coating in the upper corner of the chocolate candy melts. Let it set completely at room temperature, about 10 minutes.

6. To assemble, place the ears and tongue on the pie. Center the muzzle over the tongue, then place the chocolate-covered peanut candy on top of it for a nose. Finally, place one eye on each side of the muzzle. Refrigerate for at least 3 hours before serving.

JACK-O-LANTERN PUMPKIN PIE

MAKES ONE 9-INCH PIE

There are many things my dad and I agree on. For example, that spaghetti and meatballs is the best comfort food in the world, that you never say no to ice cream, and that pumpkin pie is happiness in a pie plate. With a silky pumpkin filling and the right touch of spice, this recipe is our go-to. And to us, pumpkin pie season is the entirety of the fall (not just Thanksgiving). I love giving it a kawaii Halloween twist with a cute jack-o-lantern face!

FOR THE PIE

1 disk Pie Crust Dough, homemade (page 122) or store-bought

1 (15-ounce) can pumpkin puree

2 large eggs, at room temperature

¾ cup sugar

1 teaspoon ground cinnamon

½ teaspoon ground ginger

¼ teaspoon ground cloves

½ teaspoon table salt

1 (12-ounce) can evaporated milk

FOR THE DECORATIONS

2 tablespoons melted chocolate candy coating

1 teaspoon melted green candy coating

½ teaspoon melted pink candy coating

1 teaspoon melted white candy coating

1. MAKE THE PIE: Preheat the oven to 425°F.

2. On a floured work surface, using a rolling pin, roll out the disk of pie crust dough into a 13-inch round. Place it in a 9-inch pie plate and crimp the edges by pinching the crust between your thumb and forefinger. Refrigerate the crust while you make the filling.

3. In large bowl, combine the pumpkin, eggs, sugar, cinnamon, ginger, cloves, and salt. Gradually whisk in the evaporated milk. Pour the mixture into the crust.

4. Bake for 15 minutes. Reduce the oven temperature to 350°F and continue to bake until the edges of the pie are set and the center is still slightly wobbly, about 45 minutes. Let the pie cool at room temperature for at least 2 hours before decorating.

5. DECORATE THE PIE: Place a sheet of parchment paper over the template (see page 234). Spoon the

melted chocolate candy coating over the parchment following the shapes of the eyes, nose, and mouth. Use a toothpick to spread the chocolate out according to the template. Repeat with the green candy coating for the stem and the pink candy coating for the cheeks. Let the coating set completely at room temperature, about 10 minutes. Then gently peel the chocolate pieces off the parchment paper.

6. On the flat side of each chocolate eye, dab a small amount of the melted white candy coating in the upper corner for a pupil. Let set completely at room temperature, about 10 minutes.

7. Place the chocolate pieces, flat side up, on top of the pie. Arrange the eyes above the nose, and place the cheeks next to the eyes. Place the mouth beneath the nose. Serve immediately or refrigerate, covered loosely with plastic wrap for up to three days.

COW ÉCLAIRS

MAKES ABOUT 18 ÉCLAIRS

As a kid, I would choose éclairs over cream puffs because I knew éclairs as "the ones with chocolate on top." While I now appreciate both equally, I still never say no to a chocolate topping. I made these éclairs extra-kawaii with adorable cow faces—perfect if you're in the "moo'd" for a crisp French pastry with a beautifully creamy vanilla filling!

FOR THE PASTRY CREAM

¾ cup sugar

6 tablespoons cornstarch

¼ teaspoon table salt

6 large egg yolks, at room temperature

3 cups milk, at room temperature

3 tablespoons unsalted butter, at room temperature

1½ teaspoons vanilla extract

FOR THE ÉCLAIRS

½ cup (1 stick) unsalted butter, at room temperature

½ teaspoon table salt

1 cup all-purpose flour

4 large eggs, at room temperature

FOR THE DECORATIONS

1 cup white chocolate chips

2 tablespoons coconut oil

About 20 pink jelly beans

About 40 mini chocolate chips

About 40 whole unsalted cashews

¼ cup semisweet chocolate chips, melted

1. MAKE THE PASTRY CREAM: In a medium-size heavy saucepan, whisk together the sugar, cornstarch, and salt. In a separate medium bowl, whisk together the egg yolks and milk. While whisking continuously to prevent lumps, slowly pour the milk mixture into the sugar mixture. Add the butter to the saucepan.

2. Place the saucepan over medium heat and cook until the butter melts and the mixture begins to thicken, about 6 minutes. Continue cooking for 1 more minute to thicken it further, stirring constantly.

3. Remove the pan from the heat and stir in the vanilla. Transfer the pastry cream to a medium bowl and press plastic wrap directly against the surface of the cream to prevent a skin from forming. Refrigerate until completely chilled, at least 2 hours.

4. MAKE THE ÉCLAIRS: Preheat the oven to 375°F. Line two baking sheets with parchment paper.

5. In a medium saucepan set over medium-high heat, bring 1 cup of water, the butter, and the salt to a boil, stirring occasionally, about 3 minutes. Reduce the heat to low, add the flour,

and stir until the mixture forms a ball, about 1 minute.

6. Transfer the dough to the bowl of a stand mixer. With the mixer running on medium speed, beat in the eggs, one at a time, mixing after each addition.

7. Scoop the batter into a large pastry bag fitted with an Ateco 867 or similar large French piping tip. Moving slowly, pipe out logs about 3 inches long and 1¼ inches wide onto the prepared baking sheets.

8. Bake until the pastries are a deep golden brown, 30 to 35 minutes. Then transfer them to a wire rack and let them cool completely.

9. Transfer the cooled pastry cream to a piping bag or a large plastic zip-top bag and cut off a medium tip. Poke two holes in the bottom of each éclair with a sharp knife, and then pipe pastry cream into the éclair in each hole until it is filled. It helps to push the tip of the piping or zip-top bag into the hole as you pipe (rather than before you start piping) to ensure that the tip of the bag is stiff enough.

(recipe continues)

The pastry cream will thicken quite a bit in the fridge and it may even look set. But if you simply stir it with a spatula before transferring it to the pastry bag, it'll have a pipeable consistency. Also, if you would like to make these éclairs ahead of time, you can prepare the shells and pastry cream, but do not fill and decorate the shells until just before serving.

10. DECORATE THE ÉCLAIRS: In a medium microwave-safe bowl, combine the white chocolate chips and coconut oil. Microwave in 20-second intervals, stirring after each interval, until the mixture is melted and smooth.

11. Dip the top of an éclair in the white chocolate mixture, shake off any excess chocolate, and place the éclair right side up on a wire rack. Let the chocolate set for about 10 seconds. Then place a pink jelly bean in the center for a nose and push the point of a mini chocolate chip into each side of the candy for eyes. Repeat with the remaining éclairs. Let the decoration set completely, about 15 minutes.

12. Use a sharp knife to cut two small holes along the long edge of the eclairs, and insert one cashew into each hole for horns.

13. Pipe small blobs of melted chocolate on top for cow spots, along with two small dots on the jelly bean for nostrils. Let set completely, about 10 minutes. Serve immediately.

PIG CREAM PUFFS

MAKES
ABOUT 24
CREAM PUFFS

Cream puffs are one of those desserts that seem complicated and fussy to make, but they're actually surprisingly easy. The batter (which is known as "choux pastry") calls for only five ingredients, and the pastry cream comes together quickly, too. I was inspired to decorate these piggies by a discovery made during my last trip to Japan: We stumbled across a creative bakery that made similar animal cream puffs, and I thought it was a genius idea to cut off the tops and add an animal face peeking in with the cream. So once I got home, these pig puffs were born!

FOR THE PASTRY CREAM

¾ cup sugar

6 tablespoons cornstarch

¼ teaspoon salt

6 large egg yolks, at room temperature

3 cups milk, at room temperature

3 tablespoons unsalted butter, at room temperature

1½ teaspoons vanilla extract

Pink gel food color

FOR THE CREAM PUFFS

½ cup (1 stick) unsalted butter, at room temperature

½ teaspoon table salt

1 cup all-purpose flour

4 large eggs, at room temperature

FOR THE DECORATIONS

2 tablespoons semisweet chocolate chips, melted

About 15 mini marshmallows, cut in half

About 60 large pink heart sprinkles

About 60 mini chocolate chips

1. MAKE THE PASTRY CREAM: In a medium-size heavy saucepan, whisk together the sugar, cornstarch, and salt. In a separate medium bowl, whisk together the egg yolks and milk. While whisking continuously to prevent lumps, slowly pour the milk mixture into the sugar mixture. Add the butter to the saucepan.

2. Place the saucepan over medium heat and cook until the butter melts and the mixture begins to thicken, about 6 minutes. Continue cooking for 1 more minute to thicken it further, stirring constantly.

3. Remove the pan from the heat and stir in the vanilla and the pink food color. Transfer the pastry cream to a medium bowl and press plastic wrap directly against the surface of the cream to prevent a skin from forming. Refrigerate until completely chilled, at least 2 hours.

4. MAKE THE CREAM PUFFS: Preheat the oven to 375°F. Line two baking sheets with parchment paper.

5. In a medium saucepan set over medium-high heat, bring 1 cup of water, the butter, and the salt to a boil, stirring occasionally, about 3 minutes. Reduce the heat to low, add the flour, and stir until the mixture forms a ball, about 1 minute.

6. Transfer the dough to the bowl of a stand mixer. With the mixer running on medium speed, beat in the eggs, one at a time, mixing after each addition.

7. Scoop the batter into a large pastry bag fitted with a medium tip. Pipe out about 1 tablespoon of batter for each cream puff, spacing them at least 3 inches apart on the prepared baking sheets.

(recipe continues)

It's important to bake the choux pastry until it reaches a deep golden brown. The shells should be light, crisp, and hollow. Otherwise, if they are underbaked, they may collapse once you take them out of the oven—and we don't want deflated piggies!

8. Bake until the cream puffs are a deep golden brown, 30 to 35 minutes. Then transfer them to a wire rack and let them cool completely.

9. Transfer the chilled pastry cream to a piping bag or a large plastic zip-top bag and cut off a large tip.

10. DECORATE THE CREAM PUFFS: Place the melted chocolate in a small plastic zip-top bag with a small corner cut off. Pipe small dots on the mini marshmallows for nostrils. Let set completely, about 10 minutes.

11. Using a serrated knife, cut each cream puff in half horizontally. On the bottom halves, pipe a generous amount of pastry cream.

12. Using a sharp knife, cut two slits in the top half of each cream puff. Insert a heart sprinkle into each slit for the ears. Put the top halves of the puffs onto the cream-filled bottom halves, angling them backward so that the pink filling shows.

13. Place the decorated mini marshmallows in the center of the filling for snouts, and then press the point of a mini chocolate chip on each side of the marshmallows for eyes. Serve immediately.

CONVERSATION HEART BREAKFAST PASTRIES

MAKES
ABOUT
14 PASTRIES

Until I turned twenty years old, I had never had one of those convenience breakfast toaster pastries. I know, I felt robbed, too! These pastries are a stepped-up version of those widely loved treats. I like to make these buttery pastries for Valentine's Day, filling them with bright red strawberry jam and dressing them up as conversation hearts. You can absolutely make them with a different flavor of jam if your Valentine prefers something else.

FOR THE PASTRIES

2 disks Pie Crust Dough, homemade (page 122) or store-bought

½ cup strawberry jam

1 large egg, at room temperature

1 tablespoon milk

FOR THE ICING

2 cups confectioners' sugar

¼ teaspoon vanilla extract

Red, pink, purple, yellow, and blue gel food colors

FOR THE DECORATIONS

About 28 mini chocolate chips

1 tablespoon chocolate chips, melted

1. **MAKE THE PASTRIES:** Preheat the oven to 375°F. Line 2 baking sheets with parchment paper.

2. On a floured work surface, using a rolling pin, roll out each disk of pie crust dough until it is ⅛ inch thick. Cut out hearts using a 2-inch-tall heart cookie cutter. Put half of the hearts on the prepared baking sheets.

3. Scoop the jam into a piping bag and cut off a small tip. Pipe about 1 teaspoon of jam onto each heart on the baking sheets, leaving a ¼-inch border. Dip your finger in water and run it along the outside edge of each heart, and then put another heart on top, pressing the edges to seal. Crimp the edges with a fork.

4. In a small bowl, whisk together the egg and milk. Using a pastry brush, brush the mixture over the pastries.

5. Bake until the pastries are golden brown on top, 18 to 20 minutes. Transfer them to a wire rack and let them cool completely.

6. **MAKE THE ICING:** In a medium bowl, whisk together the confectioners' sugar, vanilla, and 2 tablespoons plus 1 teaspoon water until smooth.

7. Transfer 2 tablespoons of the icing to a small bowl and color it red with the red gel food color. Transfer it to a small piping bag fitted with a small round tip.

8. Divide the remaining icing among four bowls and color one of each pink, purple, yellow, and blue. Transfer each color to a small plastic zip-top bag and cut off a medium tip.

9. **DECORATE THE PASTRIES:** Pipe the icing over the top of each pastry, using a single color for each (reserving the red), and spread it evenly with an offset spatula. Insert the points of two mini chocolate chips into the frosting on each pastry for eyes. Let set for about 15 minutes.

10. Pipe conversation heart messages on top of the pastries with the red icing. Use the melted chocolate and a toothpick to add smiles. Let set completely, about 10 minutes.

I recommend piping the conversations onto the hearts no more than 4 hours before you plan to serve these pastries. If left out for too long, the red icing may bleed into the pastel icing colors beneath.

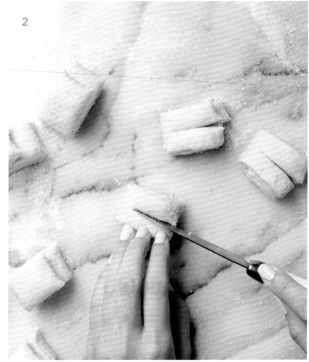

BUTTERFLY PALMIERS

MAKES ABOUT
20 PALMIERS

Palmiers are one of my mom's favorite desserts. They're a snap to make at home, thanks to store-bought puff pastry. My butterfly version is a kawaii twist on the buttery flaky cookie. With some clever cuts in the puff pastry, you can easily create the winged shape. Swapping the regular white sanding sugar for some bright colors at the end makes for a fun rainbow of butterflies that'll make your heart flutter!

¼ cup granulated sugar, plus more for the work surface

1 package (2 sheets) frozen puff pastry, thawed

Colored sanding sugar in your choice of colors

1 tablespoon chocolate chips, melted

1. Preheat the oven to 400°F. Line two baking sheets with parchment paper.

2. Sprinkle a work surface generously with white granulated sugar and put one sheet of the puff pastry on top. Evenly sprinkle the remaining ¼ cup granulated sugar over the puff pastry. Using a rolling pin, roll out the puff pastry into a 10 x 10-inch square. Fold two sides of the square into the center so that they meet in the middle. Take the same sides and fold them into the center again so that the pastry meets in the middle (see photo 1).

3. Turn the folded puff pastry onto its side so that the fold (like the spine of a book) is facing to one side. Using a sharp knife, cut the pastry into 1-inch sections. Then cut each 1-inch section down the middle from the open side (opposite the "book spine"; see photo 2), being careful to cut only three-fourths of the way to the fold. Then unfold the section to the center to form a butterfly (see photo 3). Place the butterflies on the prepared baking sheet with the fold on top.

4. Sprinkle the wings of the butterflies with the desired colors of sanding sugar (see photo 4).

5. Bake until a deep golden brown, 18 to 20 minutes. Transfer the palmiers to a wire rack and let them cool completely.

6. Repeat with the other sheet of puff pastry.

7. Transfer the melted chocolate to a plastic zip-top bag with a small corner cut off, then pipe melted chocolate on each butterfly for the antennae and a face.

If you want to change it up and make cinnamon-sugar palmiers, replace the ¼ cup granulated sugar with 2 tablespoons ground cinnamon stirred into ½ cup of sugar. Then use ¼ cup of the cinnamon-sugar to dust your work surface and ¼ cup for the inside of the palmier.

SNOWMAN CHOCOLATE CREAM PIE

MAKES
ONE 9-INCH
PIE

Despite the way the cute animated cartoons led me on as a child, I learned that building a snowman is no easy feat. They make it look so simple! But when I tried to make a snowman on a family trip to Lake Tahoe, I had to give up at the "torso with stick arms" phase. Thankfully, this pie is one snowman I *can* make. A dreamy, creamy chocolate filling is topped with a raft of whipped cream that is the perfect backdrop for a snowman face. My snowman's expression is pretty classic, but feel free to play around with yours (the Lemon Emoji Cookies on page 109 may provide some ideas!).

FOR THE PIE CRUST

1 disk Pie Crust Dough, homemade (page 122) or store-bought

FOR THE FILLING

⅔ cup sugar

3 tablespoons cornstarch

¼ teaspoon table salt

3 large egg yolks, at room temperature

3 cups milk, at room temperature

1⅓ cups semisweet chocolate chips

2 tablespoons unsalted butter, at room temperature

1 teaspoon instant espresso powder (optional)

1 teaspoon vanilla extract

FOR THE DECORATIONS

½ cup heavy whipping cream

Orange gel food color

2 chocolate candy melts

7 or 8 chocolate chips

1. **MAKE THE PIE CRUST:** Preheat the oven to 425°F.

2. On a floured work surface, roll out the pie crust dough into a 13-inch round. Press it into a 9-inch pie plate and crimp the edges. Prick the bottom of the crust with a fork, place parchment paper over the crust, and fill it with pie weights, dried beans, or rice.

3. Bake until the edges of the pie are golden brown, 12 to 15 minutes. Remove the pie weights and parchment paper, and continue baking until the bottom of the crust is a light golden brown, about 5 minutes. Let the crust cool completely.

4. **MAKE THE FILLING:** In a medium-size heavy saucepan, combine the sugar, cornstarch, and salt. In a medium bowl, whisk together the egg yolks and milk. While whisking, pour the egg mixture into the sugar mixture in a slow stream. Cook, whisking frequently, over medium-high heat until the mixture starts to bubble and thicken, 6 to 8 minutes. Reduce the heat to low and simmer, whisking frequently, until it has thickened further, 1 more minute. Whisk in the

chocolate chips, butter, espresso powder (if using), and vanilla until smooth.

5. Transfer the pudding to a separate bowl and press plastic wrap directly on the surface. Refrigerate until completely chilled, 4 to 6 hours.

6. Pour the chilled pudding into the pie crust and smooth the surface with an offset spatula.

7. **DECORATE THE PIE:** In a stand mixer fitted with the whisk attachment, beat the heavy whipping cream on high speed until stiff peaks form, about 3 minutes. Spread about 1 cup of the whipped cream on the pie, leaving a ½-inch border.

8. In a small bowl, whisk together 2 tablespoons of the remaining whipped cream with orange gel food color. Transfer it to a plastic bag with a small tip cut off. Pipe a triangle in the center of the pie and fill it in for a nose. Dab a small amount of the remaining whipped cream in the upper corner of each eye for pupils. Arrange the chocolate chips and candy melts on the pie to create the face.

GOPHER
PUDDING CUPS

I think that when many of us were young kids, we had that one special treat we would try to sneak into the grocery cart. For me, it was chocolate pudding cups. Now I like to make my own at home! I love this homemade version because I've amped up the rich chocolate flavor and piped the pudding into crisp, buttery pastry cups. Then for a spin on the "gummy worms and dirt" dessert, I nestle strawberry gophers in the Oreo "dirt," since I've always been a fan of dipped strawberries. And as it turns out, they make a great base for kawaii decorations.

MAKES
6
PUDDING CUPS

FOR THE PUDDING CUPS

⅓ cup sugar

4 teaspoons cornstarch

¼ teaspoon table salt

2 large egg yolks, at room
temperature

1½ cups milk, at room temperature

¾ cup semisweet chocolate chips

1 tablespoon unsalted butter,
at room temperature

½ teaspoon instant espresso
powder (optional)

½ teaspoon vanilla extract

1 package frozen puff pastry
shells (six 3½-inch shells total;
the shells should have a center
that's removable after baking)

FOR THE DECORATIONS

5 chocolate sandwich cookies,
such as Oreos

½ cup plus 12 individual
peanut butter chips

1 tablespoon coconut oil

6 large strawberries

1 tablespoon melted chocolate
chips

1 teaspoon melted white candy
coating

Flower sprinkles

1. MAKE THE PUDDING CUPS: In a medium-size heavy saucepan, combine the sugar, cornstarch, and salt.

2. In a medium bowl or a large measuring cup with a spout, whisk together the egg yolks and milk. While whisking constantly, pour the egg mixture into the sugar mixture in a slow, steady stream. Cook, whisking frequently, over medium-high heat until the mixture starts to bubble and thicken, 6 to 8 minutes.

3. Reduce the heat to low and simmer, whisking frequently, until thickened further, 1 more minute. Then whisk in the chocolate chips, butter, espresso powder (if using), and vanilla until smooth. Transfer the pudding to a medium bowl and press plastic wrap directly on the surface to prevent a skin from forming. Refrigerate until completely chilled, 4 to 6 hours.

4. Transfer the chilled chocolate pudding to a zip-top bag and cut off a large tip.

5. Bake the pastry shells according to the package directions. Let them cool completely. Gently remove the tops and centers of the pastry shells. Pipe the pudding into the pastry shells.

6. DECORATE THE PUDDING CUPS: Scrape the cream filling out of the cookies. Then place the chocolate cookies in a plastic zip-top bag and crush them into fine crumbs with a rolling pin. Sprinkle about 1 tablespoon of the cookie crumbs on top of each pudding to make the "dirt."

7. In a microwave-safe bowl, melt the ½ cup peanut butter chips with the coconut oil in 30-second intervals, stirring after each interval, until smooth.

8. Line a small baking sheet with parchment paper. Dip each strawberry in the peanut butter mixture, shake off any excess, and put it on the prepared baking sheet. Dip the side of one of the individual peanut butter chips into the peanut butter mixture and hold it on one side of the strawberry (to make an ear) until the chocolate sets, about 20 seconds. Repeat for the other ear. Let set completely, about 15 minutes.

9. Place the melted chocolate chips in a small plastic zip-top bag and cut off a small tip. Pipe the gopher eyes, mouth, and nose onto the strawberries. Let set, about 10 minutes.

10. Using a toothpick, dab some of the melted white candy melts at the base of the nose for the gopher teeth. Add a line in the center of the white teeth with melted chocolate to define the teeth.

11. Place one gopher in each pudding cup, along with flower sprinkles as desired. Serve immediately, or refrigerate uncovered until ready to serve.

RAINBOW FRUIT TARTS

MAKES
5 TARTS

If you're looking for a dessert on the lighter side, these rainbow fruit tarts are the treat for you. The light, crispy crust is topped with a lemon cream cheese filling that has just a touch of sweetness. The fresh fruits are so colorful that they inspired the rainbow design—and of course you can change up the rainbow depending on what you like and what's in season. One bite of these tarts and you'll be on cloud nine!

FOR THE TARTS

2 disks Pie Crust Dough, homemade (page 122) or store-bought

8 ounces cream cheese, at room temperature

½ cup sugar

1 teaspoon vanilla extract

½ teaspoon grated lemon zest

FOR THE DECORATIONS

5 large strawberries

15 canned mandarin orange slices

3 canned pineapple chunks

1 small kiwi, peeled

15 blueberries

½ cup mini marshmallows

10 semisweet chocolate chips

1 tablespoon chocolate chips, melted

1. **MAKE THE TARTS:** On a floured work surface, using a rolling pin, roll out the pie crust dough until it is ⅛ inch thick. Place a 4½-inch tart pan upside down on top of the pie crust. Using the pan as a guide, cut out five rounds of dough that are about 1 inch larger than the tart tin all around. Press each dough round into a tart tin, leaving a ½-inch overhang. Gather the dough scraps and repeat the rolling and cutting processes to create more tarts. Prick the bottom of the tarts with a fork. Freeze the tart shells for 10 minutes.

2. Preheat the oven to 375°F.

3. Bake the tart shells until they are golden brown around the edges, about 20 minutes. Let them cool for 10 minutes. Then use a sharp knife to carefully trim off the excess crust around the top of each tart.

4. In a large bowl with a handheld electric mixer, beat the cream cheese, sugar, vanilla, and lemon zest until smooth. Spread an even layer of the cream cheese filling into each tart.

5. **DECORATE THE TARTS:** Using a small knife, cut the stems off the strawberries, and then cut each strawberry crosswise into ⅛-inch-thick slices (to make round slices). Cut each slice in half to make a half-moon. Lay about 5 strawberry slices along the top of each tart.

6. Place slices of mandarin orange overlapping each strawberry layer slightly to create an inner ring.

7. Cut the pineapple chunks into ⅛-inch-thick slices, and then trim them to make rounded edges. Place the pineapple slices overlapping the mandarin orange layer to create another ring.

8. Cut the kiwi into ⅛-inch-thick slices, and then cut each slice in half to form a half-moon. Lay one kiwi slice inside each pineapple layer.

9. Center 3 blueberries on top of each kiwi slice.

10. Place 5 mini marshmallows on each side of the rainbow for clouds.

11. Press the points of two chocolate chips into the fruit on each tart to make eyes.

12. Place the melted chocolate into a small zip-top bag and pipe on smiles. Serve immediately, or refrigerate uncovered until ready to serve.

MINI TURKEY PIES

If you ever visit my hometown, you'll likely encounter three kinds of animals: dogs, cats, and turkeys. Yes, you read that correctly. There are turkeys that roam the streets alongside the morning joggers and dog walkers. I can't explain it! But they keep to themselves, and the town embraces them like a sort of widespread mascot around the holidays. These pies are inspired by those inexplicable turkeys, and they'll be right at home on your holiday table. Happy Thanksgiving!

FOR THE PIES

2 tablespoons unsalted butter, melted

⅔ cup (packed) light brown sugar

¼ teaspoon table salt

1 large egg, at room temperature

½ teaspoon vanilla extract

⅔ cup pecan halves, finely chopped

1 disk Pie Crust Dough, homemade (page 122) or store-bought

FOR THE DECORATIONS

Red, orange, and yellow candy-coated chocolates, such as M&M's

2 tablespoons chocolate chips, melted

Yellow mini candy-coated chocolates, such as mini M&M's

White confetti sprinkles

Black edible ink marker

Pink confetti quins

1. **MAKE THE PIES:** Preheat the oven to 375°F.

2. In a large bowl, using a wooden spoon, combine the butter, brown sugar, salt, egg, and vanilla. Stir in the pecans.

3. On a floured work surface, using a rolling pin, roll out the pie crust until it is ⅛ inch thick. Cut out twenty 2¾-inch rounds with a cookie cutter. Press the rounds into twenty cups of a mini muffin tin, being sure to press the crust up to the top of the cup and to smooth any folds. Scoop 1 tablespoon of the pecan pie filling into each crust.

4. Bake until the crust is golden brown and the filling is set, about 25 minutes. Let the pies cool completely in the muffin tin. Then, using a butter knife or an offset spatula, gently remove the pies from the tin.

5. **DECORATE THE PIES:** For the turkey feathers, dip the bottom of a candy-coated chocolate into the melted chocolate and press it on the top of the pie. Repeat four more times with different colors.

6. For the beak, dip a yellow mini candy-coated chocolate into the melted chocolate and press it sideways into the bottom third of the pie. If necessary, use a knife to gently carve a small slit to insert the beak.

7. Dab a small amount of the melted chocolate on each side of the beak and use tweezers to add a white confetti sprinkle on each side for the eyes. Using the black edible ink marker, add pupils to the confetti sprinkles.

8. Dab a small amount of the melted chocolate on each side of the eyes and use tweezers to add a pink confetti quin for cheeks. Let set completely, about 10 minutes.

BARS & BROWNIES

Measure the water for the icing carefully, as a few drops can make a big difference in consistency. But if you do happen to add too much, simply whisk in more confectioners' sugar, 1 tablespoon at a time, until the icing is thick enough to pipe and hold a line.

PENGUIN BROWNIES

MAKES ABOUT 11 BROWNIES

Never underestimate the power of a solid brownie recipe! Brownies are not only fantastic on their own, but they're also a great base for decorating because they're a snap to cut out with cookie cutters and dress up with a bit of icing. These penguin brownies may be reminiscent of chilly climates, but their charming bow ties and heart-shaped beaks are sure to melt even the coldest of hearts.

FOR THE BROWNIES

Cooking spray

1 cup (2 sticks) unsalted butter, melted

2¼ cups sugar

4 large eggs, at room temperature

1 tablespoon vanilla extract

1½ cups all-purpose flour

1¼ cups natural unsweetened cocoa powder

1 teaspoon table salt

1 teaspoon instant espresso powder (optional)

1½ cups semisweet chocolate chips

FOR THE ICING

1 cup confectioners' sugar

FOR THE DECORATIONS

About 11 chocolate candy melts

About 11 yellow heart sprinkles

About 22 mini chocolate chips

About 22 large heart sprinkles

About 22 yellow candy-coated chocolates, such as M&M's

1. MAKE THE BROWNIES: Preheat the oven to 350°F. Grease a 9 x 13-inch baking pan with cooking spray. Line the bottom of the pan with parchment paper, leaving an overhang on the sides to make the brownies easier to remove. If desired, use metal binder clips to hold the parchment in place on each side of the pan.

2. In a large bowl, using a wooden spoon, combine the melted butter and sugar until smooth. Add the eggs, one at a time, stirring after each addition. Stir in the vanilla. Stir in the flour, cocoa powder, salt, and espresso powder (if using). Stir in the chocolate chips. Pour the batter into the prepared pan.

3. Bake until a toothpick inserted into the center comes out clean, 30 to 35 minutes. Let cool in the pan for about 10 minutes. Then use the parchment paper to carefully transfer the brownies to a wire rack. Let them cool completely.

4. MAKE THE ICING: In a medium bowl, whisk the confectioners' sugar with 1 tablespoon of water until smooth. If the icing is too thick, add water ½ teaspoon at a time. It should be slightly thicker than liquid glue.

Transfer the icing to a piping bag fitted with a small round tip or to a plastic zip-top bag with a small corner cut off.

5. DECORATE THE BROWNIES: Using a sharp knife, cut the candy melts in half.

6. Using an egg-shaped cookie cutter (mine is 3 inches tall and 2½ inches at its widest point), cut out oval brownies for the penguin bodies. Insert the curved side of a candy melt half, at an angle, into each side of the brownies to create the wings.

7. For the penguin body, on the lower two-thirds of each brownie, pipe the outline of a large oval that touches the bottom of the brownie. On the top third, pipe an outline for another, smaller oval that touches the top of the first oval. Fill in both ovals with white icing. Place a yellow heart sprinkle in the middle of the upper oval for the nose. Insert the point of a mini chocolate chip on each side of the nose for eyes.

8. Place two large heart sprinkles end-to-end beneath the nose for a bow tie. Place two yellow candy-coated chocolates on the bottom of the brownie for the feet.

DEER BLONDIES

MAKES
ABOUT
20 BLONDIES

As much as I love a good brownie, a chewy golden blondie speckled with chocolate chips is just as satisfying. If you've never had one before, blondies are like chocolate chip cookies except that you have a whole pan of them—and the edges get nice and chewy. These deer blondies were inspired by a favorite cake I made on my YouTube channel. The chocolate eyelashes give the deer a whimsical personality, but feel free to opt for whole chocolate chips if detail work isn't your forte.

FOR THE BLONDIES

Cooking spray

2 cups all-purpose flour

2 teaspoons baking powder

½ teaspoon table salt

1 cup (2 sticks) unsalted butter, melted

½ cup granulated sugar

1½ cups (packed) light brown sugar

2 large eggs, at room temperature

2 teaspoons vanilla extract

1¼ cups mini semisweet chocolate chips

FOR THE ICING

1 cup confectioners' sugar

FOR THE DECORATIONS

40 pieces of sliced almonds

20 chocolate chips

40 mini chocolate chips

1. **MAKE THE BLONDIES:** Preheat the oven to 350°F. Grease a 9 x 13-inch baking pan with cooking spray. Line the bottom of the pan with parchment paper, leaving an overhang on the sides to make the blondies easier to remove. If desired, use metal binder clips to hold the parchment in place on each side of the pan.

2. In a medium bowl, whisk together the flour, baking powder, and salt.

3. In a large bowl, using a wooden spoon, combine the melted butter, granulated sugar, and brown sugar until well mixed. Add the eggs, one at a time, stirring after each addition. Stir in the vanilla, and then stir in the dry ingredients. Stir in the chocolate chips. Pour the batter into the prepared pan.

4. Bake until a toothpick inserted into the center comes out clean, 25 to 27 minutes. Let cool in the pan for about 10 minutes. Then use the parchment paper to carefully transfer the blondies to a wire rack. Let cool completely.

5. **MAKE THE ICING:** In a medium bowl, whisk the confectioners' sugar with 1 tablespoon of water until smooth. If the icing is too thick, add water ½ teaspoon at a time. It should be slightly thicker than liquid glue. Transfer the icing to a piping bag fitted with a small round tip or to a plastic zip-top bag with a small tip cut off.

(recipe continues)

6. **DECORATE THE BLONDIES:** Use a 2-inch round cookie cutter to cut out 20 round blondies (see photo 1).

7. Insert an almond slice in each side of the blondies for ears (see photo 2).

8. Pipe two oval shapes of icing on the bottom portion of each blondie for the deer's face. Then pipe three dots on the forehead of the deer. Press the points of two mini chocolate chips into the icing for the eyes, and press the side of a chocolate chip onto the bottom of the blondie for a nose (see photo 3). (Alternatively, omit the mini chocolate chip eyes and instead melt some of the chocolate chips and pipe out eyelashes for the deer eyes.)

BEE MILLIONAIRE SHORTBREAD

MAKES 54 BARS

This dessert is like that friend who seems to have it all together in a perfect balancing act. Texture and flavor-wise, it has everything: buttery, crumbly shortbread with ooey-gooey caramel, all coated with a layer of shiny, rich chocolate. I top them with petite bumblebees and a trail of sprinkles for a nice kawaii touch! I love adding the bees for a pop of color, and the white jimmies contrast beautifully with the deep chocolate ganache. They're sure to be a buzzworthy treat at your next party!

FOR THE SHORTBREAD

1 cup (2 sticks) unsalted butter, at room temperature

½ cup sugar

2 cups all-purpose flour

FOR THE CARAMEL

6 tablespoons unsalted butter, at room temperature

1 (14-ounce) can sweetened condensed milk

2 tablespoons light corn syrup

½ cup (packed) light brown sugar

1 teaspoon vanilla extract

1. MAKE THE SHORTBREAD: Preheat the oven to 350°F. Line a 9 x 13-inch baking pan with parchment paper, leaving an overhang on the sides to make the bars easier to remove. If desired, use metal binder clips to hold the parchment in place on each side of the pan.

2. In a large bowl, using a handheld electric mixer, combine the butter and sugar and beat on high speed until light and fluffy, about 3 minutes. Add the flour and beat on low speed until combined; the dough will be crumbly. Pour the dough into the prepared pan and, with damp hands, press it into an even layer.

3. Bake until the edges of the crust are golden brown, 20 to 25 minutes. Let it cool completely in the pan.

4. MAKE THE CARAMEL: In a medium-size heavy saucepan set over medium heat, combine the butter, condensed milk, corn syrup, and brown sugar. Cook, stirring constantly, until the mixture begins to boil, about 7 minutes. Continue to boil, stirring constantly, until the caramel begins to pull away from the sides of the pot as you stir, about 5 minutes. Be careful not to touch the caramel as it will be extremely hot. Stir in the vanilla extract. Pour the caramel over the cooled shortbread and spread it evenly with an offset spatula. Refrigerate until the caramel is completely set, about 30 minutes.

(recipe and ingredients continue)

BARS & BROWNIES

FOR THE GANACHE

½ cup heavy whipping cream,
  at room temperature

2 cups semisweet chocolate chips

FOR THE DECORATIONS

About 45 yellow candy-coated peanut
  chocolates, such as peanut M&M's

3 tablespoons chocolate chips, melted

White round confetti sprinkles

White jimmies

5. **MAKE THE GANACHE:** In a heatproof bowl or a measuring cup with a spout, microwave the heavy whipping cream in 30-second intervals, stirring after each interval, until it comes to a boil. Carefully add the chocolate chips and let sit at room temperature until the chocolate melts, about 5 minutes. Then stir until smooth. Pour the ganache over the caramel and spread it evenly with an offset spatula. Refrigerate until the chocolate is set, about 1 hour.

6. Use the parchment paper to carefully transfer the shortbread to a cutting board.

7. **DECORATE THE SHORTBREAD:** Using a toothpick, create a wood-grain texture by drawing wavy lines on the ganache. Cut the shortbread into sixths vertically and 1-inch segments horizontally to create 45 bars that are about 2 inches x 1 inch.

8. Place one yellow candy-coated peanut chocolate toward one end of each bar to make a bee.

9. Place the melted chocolate into a plastic zip-top bag and cut off a tiny corner. Pipe chocolate lines on top of each bee for the stripes, along with a small dot for the eye.

10. Tuck two white round confetti sprinkles behind each bee for wings. Use tweezers and the white jimmies to create a "bee trail."

LEMON BARS

MAKES
20 LEMON
BARS

I distinctly remember the first time I ever tasted a lemon bar. One of our family friends had made a batch for a dinner party and served them cut into cute wedges. After one bite, I was hooked on their bright, sweet, tart lemon filling atop a melt-in-your-mouth crumbly crust. Here I update the classic with another level of lemon-love by decorating them to resemble wedges of the tart fruit. They're perfectly kawaii!

FOR THE CRUST

1 cup (2 sticks) unsalted butter, at room temperature

½ cup confectioners' sugar

2 cups all-purpose flour

FOR THE FILLING

2¼ cups sugar

6 tablespoons all-purpose flour

6 large eggs, at room temperature

1 tablespoon grated lemon zest

½ cup fresh lemon juice (see note on opposite page)

FOR THE ICING

1½ cups confectioners' sugar

FOR THE DECORATIONS

40 mini chocolate chips

1 tablespoon chocolate chips, melted

Pink confetti quins

1. **MAKE THE CRUST:** Preheat the oven to 350°F.

2. In a large bowl, using a handheld electric mixer, combine the butter and confectioners' sugar and beat on high speed until light and fluffy, about 3 minutes. Add the flour and beat on low speed until combined; the dough will be crumbly. Pour the crust into a 9 x 13-inch baking pan and, with damp hands, press it into an even layer.

3. Bake until the crust is a light golden brown on top, 17 to 20 minutes.

4. **MAKE THE FILLING:** In a large bowl, whisk together the sugar and flour. Whisk in the eggs, lemon zest, and lemon juice. Then pour the filling over the crust (the crust need not be cooled).

5. Bake until the lemon bars are set, 30 to 35 minutes. Let them cool completely in the pan.

6. **MAKE THE ICING:** In a medium bowl, whisk the confectioners' sugar with 3½ teaspoons of water until smooth. If the icing is too thick, add water ½ teaspoon at a time. It should be slightly thicker than liquid glue. Transfer the icing to a piping bag fitted with a small round tip.

7. **DECORATE THE LEMON BARS:** Using a 3-inch round cookie cutter, cut out ten round lemon bars. Carefully remove them from the pan using an offset spatula, and then cut each bar in half to create a half-moon.

8. Pipe a lemon design on each bar with the icing.

9. Insert the points of two mini chocolate chips into each lemon bar for eyes. Transfer the melted chocolate to a plastic zip-top bag and cut off a small tip. Pipe on a smile using the melted chocolate. Using tweezers, place a pink confetti quin beside each eye for cheeks. (Use a small dab of icing to hold the cheeks if the lemon bar isn't tacky enough for the quins to stick.)

One lemon typically yields
3 tablespoons of juice.
I recommend picking up
3 large lemons for this recipe.

CONSTELLATION SUGAR COOKIE BARS

MAKES 30 BARS

I've always wanted to look at the stars through a telescope, except I imagine that using a telescope is like using a microscope and I never quite got the hang of those in high school (*"Uhhh . . . I see something pink and fuzzy? Oh wait, that's my finger, hold on!"*). Until I get the chance to stargaze in earnest (with help!), I'll indulge in these sugar cookie bars that are adorned with starry, sparkly constellations.

FOR THE SUGAR COOKIE BARS

2 cups all-purpose flour

1½ teaspoons baking powder

½ teaspoon table salt

¾ cup (1½ sticks) unsalted butter, at room temperature

1 cup sugar

2 large eggs, at room temperature

1 teaspoon vanilla extract

1. MAKE THE SUGAR COOKIE BARS: Preheat the oven to 350°F. Line a 9 x 13-inch pan with parchment paper, leaving an overhang on the sides to make the bars easier to remove. If desired, use metal binder clips to hold the parchment in place on each side of the pan.

2. In a medium bowl, whisk together the flour, baking soda, and salt.

3. In a stand mixer fitted with the paddle attachment, combine the butter and sugar and beat on high speed until light and fluffy, about 3 minutes. Add in the eggs, one at a time, mixing after each addition. Add in the vanilla and beat until combined. Add half of the dry ingredients and beat on low speed until combined. Scrape down the sides of the bowl. Add the remaining dry ingredients and beat on low speed until combined. Scoop the dough into the prepared pan. Using wet hands, press the dough evenly into the pan.

4. Bake until the edges are a light golden brown, about 18 minutes. Let cool in the pan for 15 minutes. Then use the parchment paper to carefully transfer the cookie to a wire rack and let it cool completely.

FOR THE FROSTING

¾ cup (1½ sticks) unsalted butter, at room temperature

2 cups confectioners' sugar

6 tablespoons natural unsweetened cocoa powder

3 tablespoons milk

½ teaspoon vanilla extract

½ teaspoon instant espresso powder (optional)

Black gel food color

FOR THE DECORATIONS

Galaxy sprinkle mix (or a combination of blue, purple, and white sprinkles)

Silver star sprinkles

White decorating icing, fitted with a small round tip (I like Wilton brand)

5. MAKE THE FROSTING: In a stand mixer fitted with the paddle attachment, beat the butter on high speed until smooth, about 1 minute. Reduce the speed to low, gradually add the confectioners' sugar and cocoa powder, and beat until combined. Scrape down the sides of the bowl. On low speed, add in the milk, vanilla, and espresso powder, if using. Beat on high speed until smooth and fluffy, about 2 minutes. Add in enough gel food color to achieve a deep black and beat until combined.

6. DECORATE THE SUGAR COOKIE BAR: Dollop the frosting on top of the cooled sugar cookie bar, and spread it evenly with an offset spatula. Scatter the galaxy sprinkle mix over the frosting. Use the silver star sprinkles to create constellations, and then connect the stars with the white decorating icing. Use more white decorating icing to pipe kawaii faces in the centers of the constellations.

7. To serve, slice the cookie into 30 equal bars.

This bar would also be a great base for piping on your and your friends' zodiac signs. Maybe this cookie can't predict the future, but it would make for one "sweet" horoscope!

FRANKENSTEIN MINT CHOCOLATE CHEESECAKE BARS

MAKES 16 BARS

Mint chocolate cheesecake has everything I love about a dessert: a smooth, decadent, creamy filling with a crunchy chocolate crust. The addition of mint extract also helps balance out the rich nature of cheesecake, giving the treat a refreshing spin. I decided to decorate these bars for Halloween because the green and chocolate color scheme reminds me of the spooky holiday. And since *Frankenstein* happened to be one of my favorite books in high-school English class, I thought these bars were the perfect contender for a not-so-spooky version of the infamous character.

FOR THE CRUST

20 chocolate sandwich cookies, such as Oreos

3 tablespoons unsalted butter, melted

FOR THE FILLING

16 ounces cream cheese, at room temperature

1 cup sugar

¼ cup heavy whipping cream, at room temperature

3 large eggs, at room temperature

1½ teaspoons peppermint extract

Green gel food color

FOR THE DECORATIONS

About 32 bone sprinkles

¼ cup semisweet chocolate chips, melted

1. **MAKE THE CRUST:** Preheat the oven to 350°F.

2. Place the chocolate sandwich cookies in a plastic zip-top bag and crush them into fine crumbs with a rolling pin. (Alternatively, pulse the cookies in a food processor until you have fine crumbs.) Transfer the crumbs to a medium bowl and stir in the melted butter. Pour the dough into an 8 x 8-inch pan with a removable bottom and, with your hands, press it into an even layer.

3. Bake until the crust is set, about 10 minutes. Let it cool in the pan while you prepare the filling.

4. **MAKE THE FILLING:** In a stand mixer fitted with the paddle attachment, combine the cream cheese and sugar and beat on medium speed until combined. Scrape down the sides of the bowl. Add in the heavy cream and beat until combined. Add in the eggs, one at a time, mixing after each addition. Scrape down the sides of the bowl. Add in the peppermint extract and beat until combined. Add in

enough green food color to achieve a light green and beat until combined. Pour the batter over the slightly cooled crust.

5. Bake until the center no longer jiggles and the edges are just beginning to turn golden brown, 35 to 40 minutes. Let cool in the pan for 15 minutes; then refrigerate for at least 2 hours.

6. Lift the removable bottom from the pan and cut the bar into 2-inch squares. If desired, level off the tops of the bars by standing them up vertically and using a sharp knife to slice downward. Do not "saw" the knife back and forth—simply push down to create a smooth surface.

7. **DECORATE THE CHEESECAKE BARS:** Insert a bone sprinkle into the sides of each bar to create bolts. Transfer the melted chocolate to a plastic zip-top bag and cut off a small tip. Pipe a face, hair , and a scar onto each cooled bar using the melted chocolate. Serve immediately, or lightly cover with plastic wrap and refrigerate until ready to serve.

MARSHMALLOW MINI CAKES

MAKES
ABOUT 15
MINI CAKES

Let's face it: sometimes you just don't have time to wait for a cake to bake! Whether you need a last-minute treat for a birthday party or you're just craving birthday cake, this recipe has your back. The addition of cake mix to the marshmallow-and-crisped-rice treats makes these taste like a chewy, crispy, delightfully sticky version of the real thing. Pop the marshmallow treats in the freezer instead of the fridge for an extra-quick "cook" time (though, for the sake of your cookie cutters, don't leave them in for *too* long).

FOR THE MARSHMALLOW TREATS

Cooking spray

4 cups mini marshmallows

¼ cup (½ stick) unsalted butter

½ cup white cake mix

5 cups puffed rice cereal

FOR THE FROSTING

1 cup (2 sticks) unsalted butter,
    at room temperature

3 cups confectioners' sugar

1 teaspoon vanilla extract

2 tablespoons milk

Pink gel food color

FOR THE DECORATIONS

¼ cup chocolate chips, melted

Rainbow sprinkles

Small heart sprinkles

Giant heart sprinkles

1. MAKE THE MARSHMALLOW TREATS: Grease a 9 x 9-inch baking pan with cooking spray.

2. In a large pot set over low heat, heat the mini marshmallows with the butter, stirring with a wooden spoon, until melted and smooth, about 4 minutes. Stir in the cake mix until combined. Then stir in the puffed rice cereal until combined. Pour the mixture into the prepared pan, and using damp hands, press it into an even layer. Refrigerate for 30 minutes.

3. MAKE THE FROSTING: In a stand mixer fitted with the paddle attachment, beat the butter on high speed until smooth, about 1 minute. Reduce the speed to low, gradually add the confectioners' sugar, and beat until combined. Add in the vanilla and milk and beat until combined. Scrape down the sides of the bowl. Beat the frosting on medium-high speed until it is light and fluffy, about 3 minutes.

4. Divide the frosting in half and color one half pink with the pink gel food color. Place the pink and white frostings into separate piping bags fitted with small star tips.

5. Turn the marshmallow treat out onto a cutting board. Cut out rounds using a 2-inch round cookie cutter for the base and a 1-inch round cookie cutter for the second tier, if desired.

6. For layer cakes, pipe a small amount of frosting on the bottom of a 1-inch round and place it on top of a 2-inch round.

7. DECORATE THE CAKES: Transfer the melted chocolate to a plastic zip-top bag and cut off a small tip. Pipe decorative stars and borders onto the cakes with the pink and white frostings, as well as decorative drips with the melted chocolate. Add sprinkles as desired. Pipe kawaii faces on the fronts of the cakes using more melted chocolate.

FROG BROWNIE BITES

MAKES ABOUT 2 DOZEN BITES

If you want a crowd-pleasing dessert, I recommend putting brownie bites at the top of your "to-bake" list. Their bite-size nature makes them perfect for parties, and the adorable frog decorations on these treats makes them extra kawaii! With just some mini marshmallow eyes, a smile, and pink confetti sprinkle cheeks, you have a confection that your friends will find "rib-beting"! Feel free to mix in chopped nuts, chocolate chips, or even diced pieces of your favorite candy.

FOR THE BROWNIES

Cooking spray

½ cup (1 stick) unsalted butter, melted

1 cup plus 2 tablespoons sugar

2 large eggs, at room temperature

1½ teaspoons vanilla extract

¾ cup all-purpose flour

½ cup plus 2 tablespoons natural unsweetened cocoa powder

½ teaspoon table salt

½ teaspoon instant espresso powder (optional)

¾ cup semisweet chocolate chips

FOR THE FROSTING

1 cup (2 sticks) unsalted butter, at room temperature

3 cups confectioners' sugar

1 teaspoon vanilla extract

2 tablespoons milk

Green and yellow gel food colors

FOR THE DECORATIONS

About 48 mini marshmallows

Black decorating icing, fitted with a small round tip (I like Wilton brand)

About 48 pink confetti sprinkles

1. MAKE THE BROWNIES: Preheat the oven to 350°F. Generously grease a mini muffin tin with cooking spray.

2. In a large bowl, using a wooden spoon, stir together the melted butter and sugar until smooth. Add the eggs, one at a time, stirring after each addition. Stir in the vanilla until combined. Stir in the flour, cocoa powder, salt, and espresso powder, if using. Then stir in the chocolate chips. Scoop the brownie batter into the prepared mini muffin tin, filling each cup three-fourths of the way full.

3. Bake until a toothpick inserted into the center of a brownie comes out clean, 13 to 15 minutes. Let them cool in the tin for about 10 minutes. Then turn the brownies out onto a wire rack and let them cool completely.

4. MAKE THE FROSTING: In a stand mixer fitted with the paddle attachment, beat the butter on high speed until smooth, about 1 minute. Reduce the speed to low, gradually add the confectioners' sugar, and beat until combined. Add in the vanilla and milk and beat until combined. Scrape down the sides of the bowl. Beat the frosting on medium-high speed until it is light and fluffy, about 3 minutes. Color the frosting lime green with equal parts of the green and yellow gel food colors. Transfer the frosting to a piping bag fitted with a large round tip.

5. DECORATE THE BROWNIE BITES: Holding the piping bag perpendicular to the brownie bite, pipe a dollop of frosting on top of each brownie bite. If a there's a peak on top of the dollop, tap the brownie bite down on the counter until the frosting smooths out.

6. Pipe black pupils in the center of the mini marshmallows and place two of them on top of the frosting on each brownie bite. Pipe smiles using more black decorating frosting. Place a pink confetti sprinkle on the side of each smile for cheeks.

It helps to cut small tips off the pastry bags or plastic bags for the brownie batter and cheesecake filling so that you can pipe them with better precision. The goal is to create thin, even layers of each, and the small tip on the brownie batter will help you cover the whole surface of the cheesecake filling so that none peeks through.

LADYBUG RED VELVET BITES

MAKES
2 DOZEN BITES

If you've never had a red velvet brownie, I recommend preheating your oven right now. These bites have that same decadent cocoa flavor we all love in red velvet cupcakes, except with the fudgy texture of a brownie. And if that doesn't entice you enough, they're also layered with a cream cheese filling that bakes up like a cheesecake surprise inside. Decorate them to look like adorable ladybugs and you have a winning dessert!

FOR THE BROWNIES
Cooking spray

½ cup (1 stick) unsalted butter, melted

1 cup sugar

¼ cup natural unsweetened cocoa powder

1 teaspoon vanilla extract

Pinch of salt

Red gel food color

2 large eggs, at room temperature

¾ cup all-purpose flour

FOR THE FILLING
6 ounces cream cheese, at room temperature

3 tablespoons sugar

1 large egg yolk, at room temperature

FOR THE ICING
1 cup confectioners' sugar

Black gel food coloring

FOR THE DECORATIONS
White decorating icing, fitted with a small round tip (I like Wilton brand)

1. MAKE THE BROWNIES: Preheat the oven to 350°F. Generously grease a mini muffin tin with cooking spray.

2. In a large bowl, using a wooden spoon, combine the melted butter, sugar, cocoa powder, vanilla, salt, and enough red gel food color to achieve a bright red and beat until combined. Add in the eggs, one at a time, mixing after each addition. Add in the flour and beat until combined. Transfer the batter to a large plastic zip-top bag and cut off a small tip.

3. MAKE THE FILLING: In a medium bowl, using a handheld electric mixer, combine the cream cheese and sugar and beat on high speed until smooth. Scrape down the sides of the bowl. Add in the egg yolk and beat until combined. Transfer the batter to a large plastic zip-top bag and cut off a small tip.

4. Pipe about 1½ teaspoons of the brownie batter into each cup of the prepared muffin tin. Pipe about 1 teaspoon of the filling over the brownie batter. Then pipe about 1½ teaspoons brownie batter on top of the filling.

5. Bake until a toothpick inserted into the center of a brownie comes out clean, 18 to 21 minutes. Let them cool in the tin for 10 minutes. Then use a butter knife or an offset spatula to gently remove the brownies from the tin and transfer them to a wire rack. Let cool completely.

6. MAKE THE ICING: In a medium bowl, whisk the confectioners' sugar with 1 tablespoon of water until smooth. If the icing is too thick, add water ½ teaspoon at a time. It should be slightly thicker than liquid glue. Color the icing black with the black gel food coloring, then transfer it to a small plastic zip-top bag and cut off a small tip.

7. DECORATE THE BITES: On the bottom part of each brownie, pipe out the base for the ladybug face using the black icing. Then add black spots and a line along the body. Let set for 20 minutes.

8. Pipe out a kawaii ladybug face on the black base using the white decorating icing.

ZEBRA CHEESECAKE-BROWNIE BARS

MAKES ABOUT
20 BROWNIES

I love a good dessert mash-up. And when it comes to combining two stellar desserts, brownie and cheesecake is an absolute winner! To tone down some of the richness of the pairing, I've made the cheesecake portion a bit lighter than most recipes so it's just a creamy, tangy note alongside the chewy chocolate brownies. And the black and white swirl on top makes the perfect base for a cute zebra! Adorable and delicious—another one of my favorite combos!

FOR THE BROWNIES

1 cup (2 sticks) unsalted butter, melted

2¼ cups sugar

4 large eggs, at room temperature

1 tablespoon vanilla extract

1 cup all-purpose flour

1¼ cups natural unsweetened cocoa powder

1 teaspoon table salt

1 teaspoon instant espresso powder (optional)

FOR THE CREAM CHEESE MIXTURE

16 ounces cream cheese, at room temperature

¾ cup sugar

½ cup all-purpose flour

2 large eggs, at room temperature

¼ cup milk, at room temperature

2 teaspoons vanilla extract

FOR THE DECORATIONS

¼ cup chocolate chips, melted

White jimmies

About 40 white chocolate chips

2 tablespoons white chocolate chips, melted

1. **MAKE THE BROWNIES:** Preheat the oven to 350°F. Line a 9 x 13-inch pan with parchment paper, leaving an overhang on the sides to make the bars easier to remove. If desired, use metal binder clips to hold the parchment in place on each side of the pan.

2. In a large bowl, using a wooden spoon, combine the melted butter and sugar until smooth. Add the eggs, one at a time, stirring after each addition. Stir in the vanilla until combined. Stir in the flour, cocoa powder, salt, and espresso powder, if using.

3. **MAKE THE CREAM CHEESE MIXTURE:** In a large bowl, using a handheld electric mixer, combine the cream cheese, sugar, and flour and beat on high speed until smooth. Scrape down the sides of the bowl. Add in the eggs, milk, and vanilla and beat until combined.

4. Spoon half of the brownie batter into the prepared pan and spread it evenly with an offset spatula. Pour the cream cheese mixture on top and spread it evenly. Dollop the remaining brownie batter on top and run a knife through the batters to create a marbled effect.

5. Bake until a toothpick inserted into the center comes out clean, 35 to 38 minutes. Let cool completely in the pan. Then refrigerate until completely chilled, at least 2 hours.

6. Use the parchment paper to carefully transfer the bar to a cutting board. Cut out rounds from the bar using a 2-inch round cookie cutter. If the brownies begin to stick to the cutter, rinse the cutter with hot water and wipe clean with a paper towel.

7. **DECORATE THE BARS:** Pipe the zebra noses, eyes, and hair on the bars with the melted chocolate. Before the noses set, use tweezers to place two jimmies on each nose for nostrils. Dip white chocolate chips into the melted white chocolate and attach one on each side of each zebra's hair for ears. (You may have to hold the chocolate chip in place temporarily so the chocolate can set, about 20 seconds.)

CAKE POP TIPS

In general, it's really easy to make cake pops, especially ones with simple shapes and minimal decorations, like my Cat Cake Pops on page 181. That said, here are a handful of tricks that will help the whole process go even smoother.

* I find that Candiquik coating is much easier to work with than candy melts when making cake pops. Even though you have to color it yourself with oil-based food color, it's worth it because candy melts burn easily and tend to be quite thick. When you dip the cake pop stick in candy coating and insert it into the cake ball, you'll notice a little ring of excess coating at the base of the ball. Wipe this off for a super-tidy finish.
* Err on the side of using less frosting. Too much frosting makes the mixture difficult to mold.
* Roll cake balls with a light touch. If you apply too much pressure, they can become misshapen.
* My favorite vessels for melting the coating for cake pops are microwave-safe silicone bowls. Silicone doesn't retain much excess heat, so once you finish dipping your pops, you can let the excess candy coating set in the bowl. Then, to reuse the candy coating another time, simply pop the hardened candy coating out of the bowl and store in a plastic zip-top bag. This makes for very easy cleanup! But if you don't have silicone bowls, use either a tall drinking glass or deep heat-safe bowl to melt the candy coating. Avoid using shallow bowls, which make it more difficult to completely submerge the cake pops in the coating.
* Make sure the cake balls are completely covered in candy coating when you dip them. If there's a small hole left uncovered (like one left by a popped air bubble), oil tends to leak out due to the moisture in the cake ball.
* To shake off the excess candy coating after dipping, do not tap the cake pop on the rim of the bowl. Instead, tap your wrist with your other hand to encourage it to drip off, letting it fall into the bowl.

CHOOSING CAKE AND FROSTING FOR CAKE POPS

Cake pops are ideal for letting your creative juices flow, not only because they can be decorated in a myriad of cute ways, but also because they work really well with homemade or store-bought cake and frosting, in all sorts of flavors. In the recipes here, you'll notice that I don't specify the types of cake and frosting to use. That's because it's entirely up to you! But I'd love to give you some ideas.

NOTES!
* Both homemade and box mix cakes will work for these cake pops, but I will say that homemade is *far* better than box mix. The texture will be much more tender and moister, and the flavors will be more balanced.
* On the other hand, homemade cake and frosting results in a denser, slightly heavier cake pop, so you will have to be gentler when dipping and decorating the pop. Just be aware!
* I recommend *avoiding* using the carrot cake and cream cheese frosting recipes in this book, both of which are delicious, but just too heavy for cake pops.

MIX-AND-MATCH
Vanilla Cake (page 29) with Vanilla Frosting (page 29)
Vanilla Cake (page 29) with Chocolate Frosting (page 35)
Lemon Cake (page 28) with Vanilla Frosting (page 29)
Cinnamon-Spiced Cake (page 81) with Vanilla Frosting (page 29)
Chocolate Cake (page 67) with Vanilla Frosting (page 29)
Chocolate Cake (page 67) with Chocolate Frosting (page 35)

CAKE POP BASICS

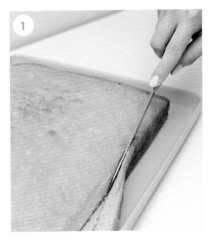

Trim edges and browning off of cake.

Place cake cubes into the bowl of a stand mixer.

Add frosting to the crumbled cake.

Roll cake balls.

Dip cake pops.

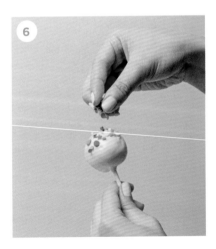

Decorate and enjoy.

CAT CAKE POPS

MAKES
3 DOZEN
CAKE POPS

If you're new to cake pop–making, these friendly felines are a great place to start. The simple oval shape and easy decorations make them ideal for even little hands to help out with. Have fun experimenting with the different color combinations as well, and you can even whip some up to mimic your own cat, if you have one. I'm "paws-itive" it would be flattered!

1 (9 x 13-inch) cake

¼ to ⅔ cup frosting

8 ounces white candy coating

72 white chocolate chips

8 ounces orange candy coating

8 ounces gray candy coating

Decorating icing in black and pink, fitted with small round tips (I like Wilton brand)

SPECIAL EQUIPMENT
36 cake pop sticks

Styrofoam block

1. Cut off the browned edges of the cake, and then cut the cake into eight pieces. Put the pieces into the bowl of a stand mixer fitted with the paddle attachment and beat on low speed to break the cake into fine crumbs, about 3 minutes. Add the frosting, 1 tablespoon at a time, until the mixture is moist enough to hold its shape when compacted. Scoop out 1½-tablespoon-size portions and roll each one into an oval shape. Place the ovals on a parchment paper–lined baking sheet.

2. In a microwave-safe bowl or tall glass, microwave the white candy coating in 20-second intervals, stirring after each interval, until melted.

3. Dip ½ inch of the ends of the cake pop sticks into the melted white candy coating and insert them into the cake ovals. Return the cake pops to the baking sheet (do not attempt to stand them up straight at this point). Let them set completely, about 10 minutes.

4. Dip the bottoms of the chocolate chips in the melted white candy coating and place one on each side of the ovals for ears. Insert the pop sticks into a Styrofoam block. Let them set completely.

5. In separate microwave-safe bowls or tall glasses, microwave the orange and gray candy coatings in 20-second intervals, stirring after each interval, until melted.

6. Working with one at a time, dip the cake pops into the desired colors of melted candy coating to fully coat them (but do not stir). Tap your wrist over the bowl to remove the excess coating, and then insert the sticks in a Styrofoam block. Let them set completely, about 10 minutes.

7. FOR COLORED EARS: Dip the ear of the cat into a contrasting color of candy coating and tap off the excess. Let set completely, about 10 minutes.

8. FOR A STRIPED HEAD: Use a toothpick to add the stripes of a contrasting color of candy coating. Let set completely, about 10 minutes.

9. Pipe on two eyes and a nose with the black decorating icing. Pipe on cheeks using the pink decorating icing.

NARWHAL CAKE POPS

MAKES 3 DOZEN CAKE POPS

To be completely honest, I didn't realize narwhals were real animals until I made these cake pops and looked online for reference photos. Can you believe it? They're practically swimming unicorns! While I may never be a marine biologist, I do know that these narwhal cake pops are "shore" to make someone's day!

1 (9 x 13-inch) cake

¼ to ⅓ cup frosting

24 ounces blue candy coating

72 mini candy-coated chocolates, such as mini M&M's

36 pieces of slivered almonds

4 ounces white candy coating

⅛ teaspoon gold luster dust

¼ teaspoon clear vanilla extract

Decorating icing in black and pink, fitted with small round tips (I like Wilton brand)

1. Cut off the browned edges of the cake, and then cut the cake into eight pieces. Put the pieces into the bowl of a stand mixer fitted with the paddle attachment and beat on low speed to break the cake into fine crumbs, about 3 minutes. Beat in the frosting, 1 tablespoon at a time, until the mixture is moist enough to hold its shape when compacted. Scoop out 1½-tablespoon-size portions and roll them into an oval shape. Place the ovals on a parchment paper–lined baking sheet.

2. In a microwave-safe bowl or tall glass, microwave the blue candy coating in 20-second intervals, stirring after each interval, until melted.

3. Dip ½ inch of the ends of the cake pop sticks into the melted blue candy coating and insert them into the bottom of the cake ovals. Return the cake pops to the baking sheet (do not attempt to stand them up straight at this point). Let them set completely, about 10 minutes.

4. Dip the ends of two mini candy-coated chocolates in the melted blue candy coating and insert the coated ends into one side of an oval to make a tail. Dip the end of a slivered almond in the melted blue candy coating and insert it into the top of the other end of the oval for a horn. Repeat for the remaining cake pops. Let them set completely, about 10 minutes.

5. Working with one at a time, dip the cake pops into the blue melted candy coating to fully coat them (but do not stir). Tap your wrist over the bowl to remove the excess candy coating, and then insert the sticks into a Styrofoam block. Let them set completely, about 10 minutes.

6. In a microwave-safe bowl, microwave the white candy coating in 20-second intervals, stirring after each interval, until melted.

7. Use a popsicle stick to apply white candy coating to the belly of the narwhals.

8. Using a food-safe paintbrush, combine the gold luster dust and clear vanilla extract in a small bowl. Paint the horns of the narwhals gold and let them dry, about 2 minutes.

9. Pipe on two eyes and a smile with the black decorating icing. Pipe on cheeks using the pink decorating icing.

EASTER EGG CAKE POPS

MAKES 3 DOZEN CAKE POPS

As a kid, my favorite holidays were always the ones associated with candy and/or dessert (think Halloween candy, Christmas cookies, Thanksgiving pumpkin pie). On Easter, I always looked forward to those sweet morsels of candy inside the Easter eggs. In fact, I would be disappointed if I ever found money inside an egg instead. My childhood self cared far more about candy in my pocket than cash in my piggy bank! With these Easter egg cake pops, you're guaranteed to hit the jackpot every time.

1 (9 x 13-inch) cake

¼ to ⅓ cup frosting

⅓ cup Easter sprinkles

8 ounces pink candy coating

8 ounces green candy coating

8 ounces lilac candy coating

8 ounces blue candy coating

Black, pink, and white decorating icing, fitted with small round tips (I like Wilton brand)

SPECIAL EQUIPMENT

36 cake pop sticks

Styrofoam block

1. Cut off the browned edges of the cake and cut the cake into eight cake pop pieces. Put the pieces into the bowl of a stand mixer fitted with the paddle attachment and beat on low speed to break the cake into fine crumbs, about 3 minutes. Beat in the frosting, 1 tablespoon at a time, until the mixture is moist enough to hold its shape when compacted. Add the Easter sprinkles and beat to combine. Scoop out 1½-tablespoon-size portions and roll them into balls. Shape them into eggs by gently rolling one side of the balls to taper them slightly. Place the balls on a parchment paper–lined baking sheet.

2. In separate microwave-safe bowls or tall glasses, microwave the pink, green, lilac, and blue candy coatings in 20-second intervals, stirring after each interval, until melted.

3. Dip ½ inch of the ends of the cake pop sticks into the desired color of melted candy coating and insert them into the bottom of the cake eggs. Return the cake pops to the baking sheet (do not attempt to stand them up straight at this point). Let them set completely, about 10 minutes.

4. Working with one at a time, dip the cake pops into the desired color of melted candy coating (it should correspond to the color used in the previous step) to fully coat them. Tap your wrist over the bowl to remove the excess candy coating. Insert the sticks into a Styrofoam block and let them set completely, about 10 minutes.

5. Pipe on kawaii faces using the black and pink decorating icing.

6. Pipe on Easter egg patterns using the white decorating icing.

FRUIT CAKE POPS

MAKES
3 DOZEN
CAKE POPS

Since fruit is good for your health and cake is good for your soul, I think we can go ahead and call these pops a superfood. So in the spirit of good health, I've transformed some of my favorite fruits into cake pop form. The shapes of these particular fruits are simple to mold. Then all it takes is a few extra moments of decoration, and you can easily form a variety of fruits that'll satisfy your sweet tooth.

1 (9 x 13-inch) cake

¼ to ⅓ cup frosting

1 ounce white candy coating

6 ounces lime green candy coating

6 ounces green candy coating

12 ounces red candy coating

8 ounces pink candy coating

½ ounce yellow candy coating

18 green mini candy-coated
    chocolates, such as mini M&M's

Decorating icing in black and pink,
    fitted with small round tips
    (I like Wilton brand)

SPECIAL EQUIPMENT
36 cake pop sticks

Styrofoam block

1. Cut off the browned edges of the cake, and cut the cake into eight pieces. Put the pieces into the bowl of a stand mixer fitted with the paddle attachment and beat on low speed to break the cake into fine crumbs, about 3 minutes. Beat in the frosting, 1 tablespoon at a time, until the mixture is moist enough to hold its shape when compacted. Scoop out 1½-tablespoon-size balls and shape them into the desired fruit as follows:

For the pear: Roll the ball into an oval, then apply pressure to the middle of the oval to create the indentation around the center.

For the apple: Roll the ball on one end to taper it slightly.

For the watermelon: Flatten the ball until it is about ½ inch thick, and then apply pressure to the sides to shape it into a wedge.

For the strawberry: Roll the ball on one end to taper it to a point.

2. Place the balls on a parchment paper–lined baking sheet.

3. In a microwave-safe bowl or tall glass, microwave the white candy coating in 20-second intervals, stirring after each interval, until melted.

4. Dip ½ inch of the ends of the cake pops sticks into the melted white candy coating and insert them into the bottom of the cake balls. Return the cake pops to the baking sheet (do not attempt to stand them up straight at this point). Let them set completely, about 10 minutes.

5. In separate microwave-safe bowls or tall glasses, microwave the lime green, green, red, pink, and yellow candy coatings in 20-second intervals, stirring after each interval, until melted.

6. FOR THE PEAR: Dip the cake pop into the melted lime green candy coating to fully coat it (but do not stir). Tap your wrist over the bowl to remove the excess candy coating, and then place a green mini candy-coated chocolate on top for a leaf. Insert the stick into a Styrofoam block and let it set completely, about 10 minutes.

7. **FOR THE APPLE:** Dip the cake pop into the melted red candy coating to fully coat it (but do not stir). Tap your wrist over the bowl to remove the excess candy coating, and then place a green mini candy-coated chocolate on top for a leaf. Insert the stick into a Styrofoam block and let it set completely, about 10 minutes. Using a toothpick, dab on some apple "shine" with white candy coating.

8. **FOR THE WATERMELON:** Dip the cake pop into the melted green candy coating to fully coat it (but do not stir). Tap your wrist over the bowl to remove the excess candy coating. Insert the stick into a Styrofoam block and let it set completely, about 10 minutes. Then dip the upper two-thirds of the pop in the melted pink candy coating and tap your wrist over the bowl to remove the excess coating. Insert the stick into a Styrofoam block and let it set

completely, about 10 minutes. Using a toothpick, dab on a line of white candy coating between the pink and green layers. Pipe on watermelon seeds using the black decorating icing.

9. **FOR THE STRAWBERRY:** Dip the cake pop into the melted red candy coating to fully coat it (but do not stir). Tap your wrist over the bowl to remove the excess candy coating. Insert the stick into a Styrofoam block and let it set completely, about 10 minutes. Using a toothpick, apply green candy coating to the top of the pop for the strawberry leaf. Use a toothpick to dot on yellow candy coating for seeds. Let it set completely, about 5 minutes.

10. Pipe two eyes and a smile onto each pop with the black decorating icing. Pipe on cheeks using the pink decorating icing.

ICE CREAM CONE CAKE POPS

MAKES
3 DOZEN
CAKE POPS

One of my favorite ways to customize cake pops is to mix sprinkles into the cake pop dough. There's something charming about biting into a pop and finding fun rainbow speckles on the inside. With these ice cream cone cake pops, I've mixed in funfetti sprinkles so they look just as cute on the inside as they do on the outside. And as for the decorations, I've opted for a Neapolitan mix here, but it would also be fun to make your own favorite flavors. Mint chocolate chip, lemon sorbet, green tea—I'm getting hungry just thinking about the possibilities!

1 (9 x 13-inch) cake

¼ to ⅓ cup frosting

⅓ cup rainbow jimmies

36 sugar ice cream cones

8 ounces white candy coating

8 ounces pink candy coating

8 ounces chocolate candy coating

36 red candy-coated chocolates, such as M&M's

Rainbow nonpareils and jimmies

Decorating icing in black and pink, fitted with small round tips (I like Wilton brand)

1. Cut off the browned edges of the cake, and cut the cake into eight pieces. Put the pieces into the bowl of a stand mixer fitted with the paddle attachment and beat on low speed to break the cake into fine crumbs. Beat in the frosting, 1 tablespoon at a time, until the mixture is moist enough to hold its shape when compacted. Add the rainbow jimmies and mix to combine. Scoop out 1½-tablespoon-size portions and roll them into balls. Place the balls on a parchment paper–lined baking sheet.

2. Using a serrated knife, carefully cut 3 inches off the top of each ice cream cone to make mini cones that are about 2 inches tall.

3. In a microwave-safe bowl or tall glass, microwave the white candy coating in 20-second intervals, stirring after each interval, until melted.

4. Dip the top of the ice cream cones in the melted white candy coating and then press the cake balls on top. Let them set completely, about 10 minutes.

5. In separate microwave-safe bowls or tall glasses, microwave the pink and chocolate candy coatings in 20-second intervals, stirring after each interval, until melted.

6. Working with one at a time, dip the cake pops in the desired color of melted candy coating and gently tap your wrist over the bowl to remove the excess. Allow some of the coating to drip down onto the cone for a "dripping ice cream" look. Let them set completely, about 10 minutes.

7. Transfer the leftover candy coating colors to plastic zip-top bags and cut off a small corner on each one.

8. Working with one at a time, pipe "syrup" drizzles over the ice cream using the candy coating in the zip-top bags, and then immediately press a red candy-coated chocolate on the very top and sprinkle the pop with rainbow nonpareils and jimmies.

9. Pipe on kawaii faces with the black and pink decorating icing.

TACO CAKE POPS

MAKES
3 DOZEN
CAKE POPS

My elementary-school self could have won an award for "Creator of the Most Boring Taco Possible." You know what my go-to order was? Ground beef in a taco shell. Thankfully (for the sake of my Mexican dining dignity), I have since graduated to more adventurous toppings. I've topped these sweet treats with coconut "lettuce," Oreo crumble "ground beef," chocolate "sour cream," and a sprinkling of "tomato" and "cheese." With their charming kawaii frosting faces, these colorful tacos are anything but boring!

1 (9 x 13-inch) cake

¼ to ⅓ cup frosting

24 ounces pale yellow candy coating

¼ cup finely chopped sweetened flaked coconut

Green gel food color

3 chocolate sandwich cookies, such as Oreos

Red and yellow jimmies

1 ounce white candy coating

Decorating icing in black and pink, fitted with small round tips (I like Wilton brand)

SPECIAL EQUIPMENT
36 cake pop sticks

Styrofoam block

1. Cut off the browned edges of the cake and cut the cake into eight pieces. Put the pieces into the bowl of a stand mixer fitted with the paddle attachment and beat on low speed to break the cake into fine crumbs, about 3 minutes. Beat in the frosting, 1 tablespoon at a time, until the mixture can hold its shape when compacted. Scoop out 1½-tablespoon-size portions and shape them into half-moons. Place the shaped cake balls on a parchment paper–lined baking sheet.

2. In a microwave-safe bowl or tall glass, microwave the pale yellow candy coating in 20-second intervals, stirring after each interval, until melted.

3. Dip ½ inch of the ends of the cake pop sticks into the melted pale yellow candy coating and insert them into the flat side of the half-moons. Return the cake pops to the baking sheet. Let them set completely, about 10 minutes.

4. Working with one at a time, dip a cake pop into the pale yellow melted candy coating to fully coat it (but do not stir). Tap your wrist over the bowl to remove the excess candy coating. Insert the stick into a Styrofoam block and let it set completely, about 10 minutes.

5. Place the coconut in plastic zip-top bag, add a drop of green food color, and shake the bag to distribute the color.

6. Remove the filling from the Oreos, then place them in a plastic zip-top bag. Crush them into fine crumbs with a rolling pin.

7. Dip the outer rim of the "taco" in the pale yellow candy coating, and then sprinkle on the colored coconut for lettuce. Using a toothpick, apply a small amount of the pale yellow candy coating on top of the lettuce, and then sprinkle the chocolate cookie crumbs over it to make the ground beef. Using tweezers, place red jimmies for tomatoes and then yellow jimmies on top for cheese.

8. In a microwave-safe bowl or tall glass, microwave the white candy coating in 20-second intervals, stirring after each interval, until melted. Using a toothpick, dab on a small amount of the melted white candy coating to make the sour cream. (For a "dolloped" look, you may have to let the candy coating set slightly at room temperature first so it's not too runny.)

9. Pipe on kawaii faces with the black and pink decorating icing.

ELEPHANT CAKE POPS

MAKES
3 DOZEN
CAKE POPS

No elephant in the room here: these pops are adorable! I love how something as simple as adding candy melts for the ears can completely transform a regular cake pop into a charming wildlife creature. Since the ears make this pop quite a bit wider, I recommend using a wide-mouth drinking glass or mug for dipping. And if you want to be extra-careful around the ears, use a spoon to scoop the gray candy coating over the pop to coat every last bit.

1 (9 x 13-inch) cake

¼ to ⅓ cup frosting

24 ounces gray candy coating

72 white candy melts

1 ounce pink candy coating

½ ounce chocolate candy coating

SPECIAL EQUIPMENT

36 cake pop sticks

Styrofoam block

1. Cut off the browned edges of the cake and cut the cake into eight pieces. Put the pieces into the bowl of a stand mixer fitted with the paddle attachment and beat on low speed to break the cake into fine crumbs, about 3 minutes. Beat in the frosting, 1 tablespoon at a time, until the mixture is moist enough to hold its shape when compacted. Scoop out 1½-tablespoon-size portions and roll them into balls. Place the balls on a parchment paper–lined baking sheet.

2. In a microwave-safe bowl or wide glass, microwave the gray candy coating in 20-second intervals, stirring after each interval, until melted.

3. Dip ½ inch of the ends of the cake pop sticks into the melted gray candy coating and insert them into the bottom of the cake balls. Return the cake pops to the baking sheet (do not attempt to stand them up straight at this point). Let them set completely, about 10 minutes.

4. Dip the bottom third of two white candy melts in the gray candy coating and insert them into each side of a ball

for ears. Repeat with the remaining white candy melts and pops.

5. Working with one at a time, dip the cake pops into the gray melted candy coating to fully coat (but do not stir). Tap your wrist over the bowl to remove the excess candy coating. Insert the stick into a Styrofoam block and let it set completely, about 10 minutes.

6. In a microwave safe-bowl, microwave the pink candy coating in 20-second intervals, stirring after each interval, until melted. Transfer the candy coating to a small plastic zip-top bag, cut off a small tip, and pipe on pink candy coating for the ear details. Use a toothpick to smooth the candy coating, if necessary.

7. Using a toothpick, dab on a backward "J" shape of gray candy coating for the elephant's trunk.

8. In a microwave safe-bowl, microwave the chocolate candy coating in 20-second intervals, stirring after each interval, until melted. Using a toothpick, dab on dots for eyes using the chocolate candy coating.

SLOTH CAKE POPS

MAKES
3 DOZEN
CAKE POPS

If I could be any animal for a day, I would want to be a sloth. Lounging around, sleeping, eating all day—the whole lifestyle sounds ideal! These pops celebrate life in the slow lane with a simple decoration that requires only two colors of candy coating. And as for the filling, I recommend a double-chocolate cake pop dough made of chocolate cake and chocolate frosting. That's my favorite flavor combination, and I often decide to use it whenever dipping chocolate cake pops.

1 (9 x 13-inch) cake

¼ to ⅓ cup frosting

24 ounces chocolate candy coating

4 ounces white candy coating

White confetti quins

SPECIAL EQUIPMENT
36 cake pop sticks

Styrofoam block

1. Cut off the browned edges of the cake and cut the cake into eight pieces. Put the pieces into the bowl of a stand mixer fitted with the paddle attachment and beat on low speed to break the cake into fine crumbs, about 3 minutes. Beat in the frosting, 1 tablespoon at a time, until the mixture is moist enough to hold its shape when compacted. Scoop out 1½-tablespoon-size portions and roll them into ovals. Place the ovals on a parchment paper–lined baking sheet.

2. In a microwave-safe bowl or tall glass, microwave the chocolate candy coating in 20-second intervals, stirring after each interval, until melted.

3. Dip ½ inch of the ends of the cake pop sticks into the melted chocolate candy coating and insert them into the bottom of the cake ovals. Return the cake pops to the baking sheet (do not attempt to stand them up straight at this point). Let them set completely, about 10 minutes.

4. Working with one at a time, dip the cake pops into the melted chocolate candy coating to fully coat

them (but do not stir). Tap your wrist over the bowl to remove the excess candy coating. Insert the sticks into a Styrofoam block and let them set completely, about 10 minutes.

5. In a separate microwave-safe bowl or tall glass, microwave the white candy coating in 20-second intervals, stirring after each interval, until melted.

6. Using a toothpick, dab on the oval-shaped base of the face using the white candy coating. Let it set completely, about 10 minutes.

7. Using a toothpick and the chocolate candy coating, dab on the brown base of the eyes by creating two lines that start from the edge of the face and extend toward the center, but that do not touch. Before the candy coating sets, use tweezers to place white confetti quins for pupils. Dab on an oval for the nose and a "W" shape underneath for the mouth using chocolate candy coating. Let set completely, about 10 minutes.

SUSHI CAKE POPS

MAKES
3 DOZEN
CAKE POPS

I thought sushi would be a great candidate to transform into cake pops because of their simple shape, iconic colors, and kawaii appeal. And what can be better than sashimi made out of gummy fish candies and California rolls made of chocolate! While I've tackled my favorites here, you can also change up the toppings just by using different colors of candy melts. And if you're feeling extra-creative, experiment with a variety of candies to come up with a whole sampler platter. Candy salmon roe, chocolate soy sauce . . . the possibilities are endless.

1 (9 x 13-inch) cake

¼ to ⅓ cup frosting

18 ounces white candy coating

6 ounces black candy coating

½ ounce green candy coating

½ ounce salmon-colored candy coating

Fish-shaped gummy candies

Decorating icing in black, white, and pink, fitted with small round tips (I like Wilton brand)

SPECIAL EQUIPMENT

36 cake pop sticks

Styrofoam block

1. Cut off the browned edges of the cake, and cut the cake into eight pieces. Put the pieces into the bowl of a stand mixer fitted with the paddle attachment and beat on low speed to break the cake into fine crumbs, about 3 minutes. Beat in the frosting, 1 tablespoon at a time, until the mixture is moist enough to hold its shape when compacted. Scoop out 1½-tablespoon-size portions and shape them as follows:

* For the onigiri: Flatten the ball until it is about ½ inch thick, and then apply pressure to the sides to shape it into a wedge.
* For the sashimi: Flatten the ball until it is about ½ inch thick, and then apply pressure to the sides to shape it into a rectangle.
* For the California roll: Roll the ball to create a short log, and then apply pressure to the top and bottom to create a slightly flattened cylinder.

2. Place the balls on a parchment paper–lined baking sheet.

3. In a microwave-safe bowl or tall glass, microwave the white candy coating in 20-second intervals, stirring after each interval, until melted.

4. Dip ½ inch of the ends of the cake pop sticks into the melted white candy coating and insert them into the bottom of the cake balls. Return the cake pops to the baking sheet (do not attempt to stand them up straight at this point). Let them set completely, about 10 minutes.

5. In separate microwave-safe bowls or tall glasses, microwave the black, green, and salmon-colored candy coatings in 20-second intervals, stirring after each interval, until melted.

(recipe continues)

CAKE POPS

6. FOR THE ONIGIRI: Dip the cake pop into the melted white candy coating to fully coat it (but do not stir). Tap your wrist over the bowl to remove the excess candy coating. Insert the stick into a Styrofoam block and let it set completely, about 10 minutes. Pipe the seaweed, two eyes, and a smile with the black decorating icing. Smooth the seaweed icing with the side of a toothpick, if necessary. Pipe on cheeks using the pink decorating icing.

7. FOR THE SASHIMI: Dip the cake pop into the melted white candy coating to fully coat it (but do not stir). Tap your wrist over the bowl to remove the excess candy coating, and then place a fish-shaped gummy candy on top before the candy coating sets. Insert the stick into a Styrofoam block and let it set completely, about 10 minutes. Pipe on the seaweed, eyes, and smile using the black decorating icing. Smooth the seaweed icing with the side of a toothpick, if necessary. Pipe on cheeks using the pink decorating icing.

8. FOR THE CALIFORNIA ROLL: Dip the cake pop into the melted black candy coating to fully coat it (but do not stir). Tap your wrist over the bowl to remove the excess candy coating. Insert the stick into a Styrofoam block and let it set completely, about 10 minutes. Dip the top of the roll in white candy coating to create rice and let it set completely, about 10 minutes. Using a toothpick, apply green and salmon-colored candy coating to the center of the rice to make the avocado and salmon. Let it set completely, about 5 minutes. Using a toothpick, apply thin lines of white candy coating to the salmon. Pipe on two eyes and a smile with the white decorating icing. Pipe on cheeks with the pink decorating icing.

CHRISTMAS CAKE POPS

**MAKES
3 DOZEN
CAKE POPS**

I loved decorating Christmas trees up until the tenth grade. That was the year I volunteered to help set up for a children's holiday party at a local historical house where they had the *most massive Christmas tree* I had ever seen in my life. And they didn't just have the one tree—it seemed like every room you walked into, there were three more smaller ones with boxes of ornaments, garlands, and lights next to them, waiting to go up. I am not exaggerating when I say I decorated Christmas trees for four hours straight that day. Nowadays I like to opt for smaller, golf-ball-size trees made of cake and chocolate. Merry Christmas to me!

1 (9 x 13-inch) cake

¼ to ⅓ cup frosting

12 ounces white candy coating

6 ounces green candy coating

6 ounces red candy coating

6 ounces chocolate candy coating

½ ounce gray candy coating

1 tablespoon light corn syrup

White nonpareils

Mini marshmallows

Gold star sprinkles

Confetti quins

Christmas sprinkle mix or holly
sprinkles

Red sanding sugar

Decorating icing in black and pink,
fitted with small round tips
(I like Wilton brand)

SPECIAL EQUIPMENT
36 cake pop sticks

Food-safe paintbrush

Styrofoam block

1. Cut off the browned edges of the cake and cut the cake into eight pieces. Put the pieces into the bowl of a stand mixer fitted with the paddle attachment and beat on low speed to break the cake into fine crumbs, about 3 minutes. Beat in the frosting, 1 tablespoon at a time, until the mixture is moist enough to hold its shape when compacted. Scoop out 1½-tablespoon-size portions and shape them as follows:

* For the puddings and polar bear: Leave the cake ball as is.
* For the Christmas tree and Santa hat: Roll the ball on one end to taper it to a point, making a cone.
* For the peppermint candy: Flatten the ball slightly to form a disk.

2. Place the shaped cake balls on a parchment paper–lined baking sheet.

3. In a microwave-safe bowl or tall glass, microwave the white candy coating in 20-second intervals, stirring after each interval, until melted.

4. Dip ½ inch of the ends of the cake pop sticks into the melted white candy coating and insert them into the bottom of the cake balls. Return the cake pops to the baking sheet (do not attempt to stand them up straight at this point). Let them set completely, about 10 minutes.

5. In separate microwave-safe bowls or tall glasses, microwave the green, red, chocolate, and gray candy coatings in 20-second intervals, stirring after each interval, until melted.

6. FOR THE SANTA HAT: Dip a cake pop into the melted red candy coating to fully coat it (but do not stir). Tap your wrist over the bowl to remove the excess candy coating. Insert the stick into a Styrofoam block and let it set completely, about 10 minutes. Using a food-safe paintbrush, brush corn syrup along the bottom rim of the hat, then dip the rim into the white nonpareils. Dip a side of a mini marshmallow in the red candy coating and place it on top of the hat.

(recipe continues)

CAKE POPS

7. FOR THE CHRISTMAS TREE: Dip a cake pop into the melted green candy coating to fully coat it (but do not stir). Tap your wrist over the bowl to remove the excess candy coating. Dip a toothpick into the green candy coating and dab on more green candy coating around the pop to create a treelike texture. Before the coating sets, place a star sprinkle at the top of the tree. Insert the stick into a Styrofoam block and let it set completely, about 10 minutes. Using a food-safe paintbrush, brush corn syrup in a spiral up the tree, and then dip the tree into the white nonpareils. Dab small amounts of the melted green candy coating onto the garland and press on confetti quins for ornaments.

8. FOR THE PUDDING: Dip a cake pop into the melted chocolate candy coating to fully coat it (but do not stir). Tap your wrist over the bowl to remove the excess candy coating. Insert the stick into a Styrofoam block and let it set completely, about 10 minutes. Using a toothpick, dab white candy coating on top of the pudding and create drips. Place the Christmas sprinkle mix or holly sprinkles on top with tweezers.

9. FOR THE POLAR BEAR: Dip a cake pop into the melted white candy coating to fully coat it (but do not stir). Tap your wrist over the bowl to remove the excess candy coating, and then place two mini marshmallows on the top of the pop for ears. Insert the stick into a Styrofoam block and let it set completely, about 10 minutes. Use a toothpick to dab on gray candy coating for the muzzle.

10. FOR THE PEPPERMINT CANDY: Dip a cake pop into the melted white candy coating to fully coat it (but do not stir). Tap your wrist over the bowl to remove the excess candy coating. Insert the stick into a Styrofoam block and let it set completely, about 10 minutes. Using a food-safe paintbrush, brush on corn syrup in a swirl pattern. Dip the pop in the red sanding sugar and then gently remove any excess with a toothpick.

11. Pipe kawaii faces on all the pops using the black and pink decorating icings.

These pops are best enjoyed immediately, as the chocolate coating can crack if it is returned to the freezer.

ZOO ANIMAL BANANA POPS

MAKES
10 BANANA
POPS

Frozen bananas are that classic treat on those days of "Well, if it's mostly a banana, this counts as a nutritious snack, right? And didn't someone say dark chocolate is good for you?" Except I find myself in that mood every day, and then sometimes I get a chocolate cupcake afterward, too, because the banana didn't count as dessert. These pops take the treat to a whole new level with their adorable animal decorations. The smooth chocolate coating makes a great canvas for creating your favorite wildlife creatures, so have fun with your imagination and snack to your heart's content!

FOR THE BANANA POPS
5 large bananas

1 cup semisweet chocolate chips

6 tablespoons coconut oil

1 cup peanut butter chips

1 cup white chocolate chips

FOR THE POLAR BEAR
Mini marshmallows

FOR THE CAT
Peanut butter chips

Semisweet chocolate chips

FOR THE MONKEY
Soft caramels

Semisweet chocolate chips

Banana candies

FOR THE ZEBRA
Semisweet chocolate chips

FOR ALL POPS
Giant heart sprinkles

Flower sprinkles

SPECIAL EQUIPMENT
10 popsicle sticks

1. Peel the bananas and cut them in half crosswise. Insert a popsicle stick into the cut end of each banana half. Freeze the bananas for at least 30 minutes.

2. In a bowl or tall microwave-safe drinking glass, microwave the semisweet chocolate chips and 2 tablespoons of the coconut oil together in 20-second intervals, stirring after each interval, until melted. Repeat for the peanut butter and white chocolate chips (separately).

3. **FOR THE POLAR BEAR:** Dip a frozen banana pop into the white chocolate coating until it is fully submerged. Remove the pop and gently tap it against the side of the glass to remove any excess coating. Let it set completely, about 1 minute. Then dip six mini marshmallows into the melted white chocolate coating and press them onto the pop for ears, arms, and legs. Cut one mini

marshmallow in half and dip the sticky side into the melted white chocolate coating. Press it onto the banana pop for a nose. Use a toothpick to dab on melted semisweet chocolate coating for eyes and the nose.

4. **FOR THE CAT:** Dip a frozen banana pop into the peanut butter–chocolate coating until it is fully submerged. Remove the pop and gently tap it against the side of the glass to remove any excess coating. Let it set completely, about 1 minute. Dip four peanut butter chips into the melted peanut butter–chocolate coating and press them onto the pop for the arms and legs (flat sides facing outward). Dip the flat side of another peanut butter chip into the melted peanut butter–chocolate coating and press it onto the top of the pop for an ear; then repeat with a semisweet chocolate chip for the other ear. Use a toothpick dipped in the semisweet chocolate coating to dot on a face.

(recipe continues)

5. **FOR THE MONKEY:** Dip a frozen banana pop into the semisweet chocolate coating until it is fully submerged. Remove the pop and gently tap it against the side of the glass to remove any excess coating. Let it set completely, about 1 minute. Dip six semisweet chocolate chips into the melted semisweet chocolate coating and press them onto the pop for the ears, arms, and legs (flat sides facing outward). Mold a soft caramel into an oval for the face, and then press it onto the surface of the pop. Use a toothpick dipped in the semisweet chocolate coating to dot on a face. Dip a banana candy into the melted semisweet candy coating and press it onto the end of one arm.

6. **FOR THE ZEBRA:** Dip a frozen banana pop into the white chocolate coating until it is fully submerged. Remove the pop and gently tap it against the side of the glass to remove any excess coating. Let it set completely, about 1 minute. Dip a toothpick into the melted semisweet chocolate coating and drag it across the surface of the pop to create stripes. Dip six semisweet chocolate chips into the melted white chocolate coating and press them onto the pop for the ears, arms, and legs (flat sides facing outward). Use a toothpick dipped in the semisweet chocolate coating to dot on a muzzle and eyes. Let it set, about 1 minute. Dip another toothpick in the white chocolate coating and dot a nose on the muzzle.

7. Repeat with the remaining ingredients to make more of the animals of your choice.

8. Decorate all the pops with additional heart or flower sprinkles, as desired, by dipping them into the matching color of chocolate coating and pressing them onto the pop.

CANDY & OTHER SWEETS

EDIBLE COOKIE DOUGH BITES

MAKES 1 DOZEN BITES

If you've never eaten cookie dough straight from the bowl, you're either a liar or someone with impeccable self-control. I can't resist sneaking a spoonful despite what they say about raw eggs, so this recipe has become one of my favorites. These bites were inspired by recent trends in ready-to-eat cookie dough, and they taste just like the real deal. And with little kawaii faces and sprinkle accessories, they're even harder to resist.

FOR THE COOKIE DOUGH

1 cup all-purpose flour

½ cup (1 stick) unsalted butter, at room temperature

6 tablespoons granulated sugar

6 tablespoons (packed) light brown sugar

1 teaspoon vanilla extract

2 tablespoons milk, at room temperature

¼ teaspoon table salt

½ cup mini chocolate chips

FOR THE DECORATIONS

1 tablespoon chocolate chips, melted

About 24 mini chocolate chips

Confetti quins

Heart and flower sprinkles

1. MAKE THE COOKIE DOUGH: Preheat the oven to 350°F. Line a small baking sheet with parchment paper.

2. Sprinkle the flour over the prepared baking sheet and bake until it is a light golden brown, about 8 minutes. Let it cool completely. This will make the flour safe to consume.

3. In a large bowl, using a handheld electric mixer, combine the butter, granulated sugar, and brown sugar and beat on high speed until light and fluffy, about 3 minutes. Add in the vanilla and milk and beat until combined. Add in the toasted flour and the salt and beat until combined. Then add in the mini chocolate chips and beat to combine. Scoop out 1-tablespoon-size balls, roll them in your hands until smooth, and place them into mini-cupcake liners. Using the bottom of a glass, flatten each ball slightly.

4. DECORATE THE BITES: Place the melted chocolate chips in a plastic zip-top bag and cut off a small corner.

5. Pipe smiles onto the bites with the melted chocolate, and then place a mini chocolate chip, point down, on each side of the smile for the eyes. Press a pink confetti quin beside each

eye for cheeks. Top the bites with heart, flower, and confetti quin sprinkles.

VARIATIONS

While this recipe is for classic chocolate chip cookie dough, I have some tasty variations to share, too:

PEANUT BUTTER CUP DOUGH: Add 3 tablespoons peanut butter to the wet ingredients. Beat in the flour and salt, and then fold in two chopped peanut butter cups at the end.

UNICORN SUGAR COOKIE DOUGH: Omit the brown sugar and add 5 more tablespoons granulated sugar to the wet ingredients. Scoop heaping tablespoons of the dough into three separate bowls and use gel food colors to dye one pink, one blue, and the third purple. Swirl the colored dough into the sugar cookie dough along with 1 tablespoon of sprinkles.

CHOCOLATE HAZELNUT S'MORES DOUGH: Add 3 tablespoons chocolate hazelnut spread (such as Nutella) to the wet ingredients and reduce the granulated sugar by 2 tablespoons. After adding the flour and salt, stir in ¼ cup mini marshmallows and ¼ cup chopped graham crackers.

BUNNY & CARROT MERINGUES

MAKES 20 MERINGUES

Meringues are a completely underrated treat. They're light as air, with a satisfying crisp *snap* the moment you bite into one. Then they melt in your mouth like a dainty kiss of vanilla cotton candy. Amazing! These bunny and carrot meringues are a kawaii take on the classy treat.

4 large egg whites

¼ teaspoon cream of tartar

¼ teaspoon vanilla extract

¼ teaspoon table salt

1 cup sugar

Black, pink, green, and orange gel food colors

> Whenever I'm working with egg whites, I like to separate each egg into a separate small bowl before adding it to my larger bowl. This way, if I break a yolk, I don't mess up the entire mixture!

1. Preheat the oven to 225°F. Line two baking sheets with parchment paper.

2. In a stand mixer fitted with the whisk attachment, combine the egg whites, cream of tartar, vanilla, and salt and beat on high speed until foamy, about 1 minute. Reduce the speed to low and gradually add the sugar. Then increase the speed to high and beat until stiff, glossy peaks form, about 7 minutes.

3. Transfer ¼ cup of the meringue to a separate bowl and dye it black with the black gel food color. Transfer it to a small piping bag fitted with a small round tip or to a small plastic zip-top bag and cut off a small tip.

4. Transfer ¼ cup of the remaining meringue to a separate bowl and dye it pink with the pink gel food color. Transfer it to a small piping bag fitted with a small round tip or to a small plastic zip-top bag and cut off a small tip.

5. Transfer ⅓ cup of the remaining meringue to a separate bowl and dye it green with the green gel food color. Transfer it to a small piping bag fitted with a small round tip or to a small plastic zip-top bag and cut off a small tip.

6. Transfer ½ cup of the remaining meringue to a separate bowl and dye it orange with the orange gel food color. Transfer it to a piping bag fitted with a medium round tip or to a plastic zip-top bag and cut off a medium tip.

7. Transfer the remaining white meringue to a piping bag fitted with a medium round tip or to a plastic zip-top bag and cut off a medium tip.

8. For the bunnies, onto one of the prepared baking sheets, use the white meringue to pipe oval shapes for the faces and two longer ovals on top of the faces for ears. Pipe the inner part of the ears with the pink meringue, and pipe on a kawaii face with the black meringue.

9. For the carrots, onto the other prepared baking sheet, pipe triangles with the orange meringue using a zigzag motion, starting from the widest part of the carrot and working downward to a point. Pipe a stem on top with the green meringue, and then pipe on a kawaii face with the black meringue.

10. Bake until the meringues can be removed from the baking sheet without leaving any residue, about 1 hour and 30 minutes. Let them cool completely on the baking sheets before serving.

If you use my recipe for soft caramel on page 223, make the caramel up to the point before you pour it into the pan. Let it set in the bowl until it is thick but still pourable, about 5 minutes, and it's ready to make turtles.

Chocolate Turtle Turtles

MAKES ABOUT
3 DOZEN
TURTLES

The cheeseball in me could not pass up on the opportunity to create chocolate turtle *turtles*. It's just too perfect! However, I assure you that my motivation to whip up this recipe extends beyond bad puns. These chocolate turtles are simple to put together with an addicting mix of salted toasted pecans, chewy golden caramel, and just a kiss of chocolate on top. They make a fantastic gift for any friend with a sweet tooth and good sense of humor!

FOR THE TURTLES

3 cups salted roasted pecan halves

1 recipe Kawaii Microwave Caramels (see page 223 and note on opposite page), or 36 store-bought soft caramels

1¼ cups semisweet chocolate chips

FOR THE DECORATIONS

2 ounces white candy coating, melted (about 2 tablespoons melted candy coating)

Confetti quins

Black edible ink marker

1. **MAKE THE TURTLES:** Line two baking sheets with parchment paper. Arrange clusters of five pecan halves in a starlike pattern on the baking sheets.

2. If you are using store-bought caramels, put them in a microwave-safe bowl or measuring cup with a spout and microwave in 20-second intervals, stirring after each interval, until melted.

3. Gently pour or spoon about 1 teaspoon of the caramel (homemade or store-bought) over the center of each pecan cluster to connect all the pecans. Let the caramel set completely at room temperature, about 15 minutes.

4. In a microwave-safe bowl, microwave the chocolate chips in 30-second intervals, stirring after each interval, until melted. Gently pour or spoon about ½ teaspoon of the melted chocolate over each portion of caramel and spread it out with the back of a spoon. Let the chocolate set completely at room temperature, about 10 minutes.

5. **DECORATE THE TURTLES:** Place the melted white candy coating in a plastic zip-top bag and cut off a small tip. Ensure that the candy coating is thick enough to pipe by piping a test flower on a sheet of parchment paper. If the coating is too runny, let it set at room temperature for 1 minute, then try again. Continue to let the coating set until it's pipeable. Pipe flowers on top of the chocolate turtle shells, and then use tweezers to place a confetti quin in the center of each flower.

6. Pipe two dots of white candy coating on the front of one pecan half for eyes. Let set completely, about 10 minutes.

7. Using the black edible ink marker, draw on pupils for the eyes.

MERMAID MINT ICE CREAM

MAKES
3 PINTS

One of my favorite summer discoveries was a recipe for no-churn ice cream. When I tried it out, I was amazed at how smooth, creamy, and refreshing it was. I also love that customizing it is super-easy—just swap the mint extract for vanilla, toss in your favorite toppings, and you have your own custom ice cream. Here I also color the ice cream base and create a marbled effect that reminds me of the ocean. With some chocolate mermaid tails, graham cracker sand, and sprinkle starfish, you have a treat that'll make you never want to "wave" goodbye to summer!

FOR THE ICE CREAM

2 cups heavy whipping cream, cold

1 teaspoon peppermint extract

1 (14-ounce) can sweetened condensed milk

Mint green, teal, and purple gel food colors

FOR THE DECORATIONS

1 ounce blue candy coating

1 ounce purple candy coating

1 ounce white candy coating

½ ounce melted chocolate candy coating

Gold star sprinkles

Crushed graham crackers

SPECIAL EQUIPMENT

Mermaid tail silicone candy mold (can be purchased online)

Seashell silicone mold (can be purchased online and in some craft stores)

1. In a stand mixer fitted with the whisk attachment, beat the cream on high speed until stiff peaks form, about 3 minutes. Pour in half of the condensed milk, and using a rubber spatula, fold until combined. Fold in the remaining condensed milk and the peppermint extract until combined. Divide the mixture among four bowls. Leave one bowl white, then color one bowl mint green, another teal, and the third purple with the gel food colors.

2. Alternating colors, dollop the four colors of the mixture, 2 tablespoons at a time, into a 6-cup freezer-safe container. Swirl the colors with a butter knife, being careful not to blend them too much. Cover and freeze until firm, at least 6 hours.

3. DECORATE THE ICE CREAM AND ASSEMBLE TWO SUNDAES: In a microwave-safe bowl, microwave the blue candy coating in 30-second intervals, stirring after each interval, until melted. Spoon the coating into a mermaid tail candy mold and let it set completely in the refrigerator, about 15 minutes. Then carefully remove the tail from the mold, and wash and dry the mold. Repeat with the purple candy coating to create a second tail.

4. In a microwave-safe bowl, microwave the white candy coating in 30-second intervals, stirring after each interval, until melted. Spoon the melted coating into seashell candy molds. Refrigerate until set completely, about 15 minutes.

5. Gently remove the seashells from the molds.

6. Using a toothpick, add kawaii faces to the seashells with the melted chocolate coating and let them set, about 5 minutes.

7. Using an ice cream scoop, scoop the ice cream into two sundae glasses. Decorate with the seashells, mermaid tails, sprinkles, and graham cracker crumbs.

KAWAII-STYLE CHOCOLATE TRUFFLES

MAKES 18 TRUFFLES

Everyone's ears seem to perk up when they hear the words "chocolate truffles." There's just something fancy and indulgent-sounding in the name. But guess what? Truffles are composed of just two ingredients, and they're a breeze to make at home. Best of all, this means you're free to customize to your heart's content. Kawaii faces and brightly colored sprinkles were my picks here, but cocoa powder, shredded coconut, and white chocolate drizzle would also be fun.

FOR THE TRUFFLES

1⅓ cups semisweet chocolate chips

½ cup heavy whipping cream

FOR THE DECORATIONS

Rainbow sprinkles

Chopped unsalted peanuts

12 ounces chocolate candy coating

½ ounce white candy coating

½ ounce pink candy coating

1. MAKE THE TRUFFLES: Place the chocolate chips in a heatproof bowl.

2. In a small saucepan set over medium heat, heat the cream, stirring it frequently, until it begins to simmer, 5 minutes. Pour the cream over the chocolate chips and let sit for about 5 minutes. Then stir until smooth. Cover with plastic wrap and refrigerate until firm, about 2 hours.

3. Line a baking sheet with parchment paper.

4. Scoop out 1½-tablespoon-size portions of the chocolate mixture and roll them into balls. Place the balls on the prepared baking sheet and refrigerate until firm, about 30 minutes.

5. DECORATE THE TRUFFLES: For the sprinkle-covered truffles, roll the truffles in a plate of rainbow sprinkles until completely covered.

6. For the peanut-covered truffles, roll the truffles in a plate of chopped peanuts until completely covered.

7. For the kawaii face truffles, line a baking sheet with parchment paper.

8. In a microwave-safe bowl, microwave the chocolate candy coating in 30-second intervals, stirring after each interval, until smooth. Hold a truffle on top of the tines of the fork, dip it into the melted candy coating, and tap off any excess chocolate. Transfer the truffle to the prepared baking sheet. Repeat with the remaining truffles. Let them set completely, about 10 minutes.

9. In separate microwave-safe bowls, microwave the white and pink candy coatings in 30-second intervals, stirring after each interval, until smooth. Transfer the melted coatings to separate small plastic zip-top bags and cut off a small tip. Pipe on eyes and mouths with the white candy coating, and pipe on cheeks with the pink candy coating.

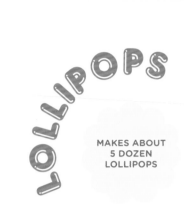

LOLLIPOPS

**MAKES ABOUT
5 DOZEN
LOLLIPOPS**

As a kid, my favorite flavor of lollipop was always "butterscotch," which I later found out is essentially "sugar-flavored." Go figure. These pretty pops are an upgraded version of the classic, with a gorgeous clear (and unflavored) candy base flecked with colorful sprinkles. Leave them as is or feel free to add your favorite flavor: simply mix in 1½ teaspoons of a flavored extract after pouring the mixture into the heatproof measuring cup.

FOR THE LOLLIPOPS
2 cups sugar

⅔ cup light corn syrup

FOR THE DECORATIONS
Sprinkles

Candies of your choice

SPECIAL EQUIPMENT
Lollipop sticks

1. Line two baking sheets with parchment paper.

2. In a heavy saucepan set over medium heat, combine the sugar, corn syrup, and ⅓ cup of water. Attach a candy thermometer to the inside of the saucepan. Increase the heat to medium-high and bring the mixture to a boil. Stir until the sugar has dissolved. Using a pastry brush dipped in water, brush down the sides of the pan to prevent crystallization. Boil until the mixture registers 310°F on the candy thermometer, 5 to 7 minutes. Pour the mixture directly into a spouted heatproof measuring cup. Be careful not to touch the sugar syrup as it will be extremely hot.

3. Working with two lollipops at a time, pour rounds of the sugar syrup that are 1½ to 2 inches in diameter onto a prepared baking sheet. Immediately press a lollipop stick into each one, and then rotate the lollipop stick halfway to cover the top of the stick. Decorate the syrup with sprinkles and any desired candies.

4. Let the lollipops harden at room temperature, about 5 minutes.

If the sugar syrup hardens too much while you are making the lollipops, place the measuring cup on a microwave-safe plate (to catch any drips) and microwave in 30-second intervals, stirring after each interval, until it is liquid again.

KAWAII MICROWAVE CARAMELS

MAKES ABOUT 4 DOZEN CARAMELS

Even though these caramels are made in the microwave, they have all the rich flavor and creamy texture of the traditional treat—just with less hassle. There are few more satisfying things than taking a bite of one of these caramels and seeing that ooey-gooey stretch as you pull your hand away! Here I've given these soft caramels a kawaii makeover. I press flower sprinkles into some of these candies, but you can easily customize them to suit any occasion or holiday. Or if you want to keep it simple, draw a kawaii face onto the wrapper with an edible ink marker and you have an easy, adorable, crowd-pleasing treat.

FOR THE CARAMELS
Cooking spray

¼ cup (½ stick) unsalted butter, at room temperature

½ cup (packed) light brown sugar

½ cup granulated sugar

½ cup light corn syrup

½ cup sweetened condensed milk

¼ teaspoon table salt

FOR THE DECORATIONS
Sprinkles (optional)

Black edible ink marker

1. Spray an 8 x 8-inch baking pan with cooking spray.

2. In a large microwave-safe bowl, combine the butter, brown sugar, granulated sugar, corn syrup, condensed milk, and salt. Microwave in 2-minute intervals, stirring after each interval, until melted, about 6 minutes total. Be careful; the mixture will be extremely hot. Pour the caramel into the prepared baking pan and let it cool for 15 minutes. Then refrigerate until firm, about 30 minutes.

3. Turn the pan upside down onto a cutting board and gently remove the caramel. Using a knife sprayed with cooking spray, cut the caramel into sixths vertically and into eighths horizontally, making about forty-eight 1¼ x 1-inch rectangles. Press sprinkles on top to decorate, if desired.

4. Wrap the caramels in wax paper. Draw kawaii faces on the wrappers with the edible ink marker.

COFFEE FLAVORED DOUGHNUT MARSHMALLOWS

MAKES ABOUT 35 MARSHMALLOWS

Homemade marshmallows are one of my all-time favorite desserts to make. It never fails to impress someone when you surprise them with a bag of huge, fluffy clouds of marshmallow and then tell them they're *homemade*. To mix up the flavor, swap the coffee for room temperature water and add 1 teaspoon of the extract of your choice (peppermint is one of my favorites for the holidays!). But I do love this pairing of coffee marshmallows and doughnut decorations. With their colorful sprinkles, glossy icing, and cute faces, they're a kawaii take on the classic doughnuts and coffee.

FOR THE MARSHMALLOWS
Cooking spray

½ cup cornstarch

½ cup confectioners' sugar

1 cup coffee, at room temperature

3 (3¼-ounce) envelopes unflavored gelatin (about 7½ teaspoons)

½ cup light corn syrup

2 cups granulated sugar

½ teaspoon table salt

1 teaspoon instant espresso powder

2 tablespoons vanilla extract

FOR THE ICING
1 cup confectioners' sugar

Pink gel food color

1 teaspoon natural unsweetened cocoa powder

FOR THE DECORATIONS
Rainbow nonpareils and jimmies

Black decorating icing, fitted with a small round tip (I like Wilton brand)

1. **MAKE THE MARSHMALLOWS:** Grease a 9 x 13-inch baking pan with cooking spray.

2. In a medium bowl, whisk together the cornstarch and confectioners' sugar. Set aside.

3. In a stand mixer fitted with the whisk attachment, beat ½ cup of the coffee and the gelatin on low speed until combined. Allow the gelatin to bloom, about 5 minutes.

4. Meanwhile, in a heavy saucepan set over medium-high heat, combine the remaining ½ cup coffee with the corn syrup, granulated sugar, and salt. Attach a candy thermometer to the side of the pan and heat until the mixture registers 240°F. Do not stir it.

5. With the mixer running on medium speed, drizzle the hot sugar syrup down the side of the bowl and into the gelatin mixture. Beat for 30 seconds. Then increase the speed to high and beat until stiff peaks form, about 8 minutes. Reduce the speed to medium and beat in the espresso powder until combined. Gradually beat in the vanilla until combined.

6. Working quickly, pour the mixture into the prepared baking pan and smooth it with an offset spatula. Sift some of the cornstarch mixture over the top of the marshmallows. Cover loosely with plastic wrap, then let them set in the pan at room temperature for at least 6 hours or overnight.

7. Sift the remaining cornstarch mixture over a work surface. Turn the marshmallow slab out onto the surface, then flip the slab over so both sides are covered in the cornstarch mixture. Cut out rounds using a 1½-inch round cookie cutter. You may have to dip the cookie cutter in the cornstarch mixture to help prevent sticking.

8. **MAKE THE ICING:** In a medium bowl, whisk the confectioners' sugar with 1 tablespoon of water. Transfer half of the icing to a separate bowl. Dye one half pink with the gel food color and the other half brown with the cocoa powder. Transfer the icings to plastic zip-top bags with small tips cut off.

9. **DECORATE THE MARSH-MALLOWS:** Pipe the pink and brown icings onto the marshmallows. Top with the rainbow sprinkles. Let set completely, 30 minutes. Pipe on kawaii faces with the black decorating icing.

CANDY & OTHER SWEETS

HEDGEHOG FUDGE

MAKES
ABOUT
64 PIECES

Chocolate fudge is a must-have recipe for your repertoire because of how easy and delicious it is. In fact, it requires only four ingredients! Just melt, mix, and pour, and you have a great base for some kawaii decorations. Because of the inherently bumpy surface of this fudge, I thought I'd go ahead and amp up the texture. So I use a fork to make it especially rugged to mimic a hedgehog's needled back, and then I finished it off with a piped chocolate face. The combination of rich chocolate, buttery walnuts, and peanut butter makes for a real gem of a recipe—or should I say "needle" —in the haystack!

FOR THE FUDGE

3 cups semisweet chocolate chips

1 (14-ounce) can sweetened condensed milk

1 cup chopped walnuts

1 teaspoon vanilla extract

FOR THE DECORATIONS

¼ cup peanut butter chips, melted

1 tablespoon melted chocolate chips

1. **MAKE THE FUDGE:** Line an 8 x 8-inch baking pan with parchment paper, leaving an overhang on the sides to make the fudge easier to remove.

2. In a medium-size heavy saucepan set over medium heat, combine the chocolate chips and condensed milk and heat, stirring with a wooden spoon, until completely smooth, about 3 minutes. Remove the pan from the heat. Stir in the walnuts and vanilla. Pour the mixture into the prepared baking pan and smooth it with a spatula. Let it set completely in the refrigerator, about 2 hours.

3. Cut out rounds of fudge using a 1-inch round cookie cutter. Using a fork, scrape rough lines onto each round to mimic hedgehog spines.

4. **DECORATE THE FUDGE:** Place the melted peanut butter chips in a plastic zip-top bag and cut off a small tip. Pipe the peanut butter on the lower third of the fudge for the faces. Let set completely, about 10 minutes.

5. Using a toothpick, dab on the melted chocolate for hedgehog eyes and noses. Let set completely, about 10 minutes.

BEAR PEANUT BUTTER CUPS

MAKES 20 PEANUT BUTTER CUPS

If there's one candy that defined my sweet tooth as a child, it's peanut butter cups. In fact, I used to snack on them in secret and hide the wrappers in my room (sorry, Mom and Dad!). With this recipe, I decided to give the cups a kawaii makeover, since the round shape and smooth base makes them ideal for piped chocolate decorations. But if you're in a hurry, a smattering of rainbow sprinkles always makes for a cute treat in a pinch.

FOR THE PEANUT BUTTER CUPS

2½ cups semisweet
    chocolate chips

⅔ cup creamy peanut butter
    (not natural; see note on
    page 103)

3 tablespoons unsalted butter,
    at room temperature

⅔ cup confectioners' sugar

FOR THE DECORATIONS

About 40 semisweet
    chocolate chips

1 tablespoon melted white
    candy coating

1 tablespoon melted black
    candy coating

1 tablespoon melted pink
    candy coating

1.   Line a muffin tin with twenty paper or silicone cupcake liners.

2.   In a microwave-safe bowl, microwave the chocolate chips in 20-second intervals, stirring after each interval, until smooth. Spoon 1 teaspoon of the melted chocolate into the bottom of each liner, tapping the tin on the counter to smooth the chocolate if necessary. Refrigerate until set, about 15 minutes. Reserve the remaining melted chocolate.

3.   Meanwhile, in a medium bowl, using a handheld electric mixer, combine the peanut butter, butter, and confectioners' sugar and beat on high speed until smooth, about 2 minutes. Transfer the mixture to a piping bag and cut off a medium tip. Pipe about 1 tablespoon of the peanut butter mixture into each chilled chocolate cup. Refrigerate for 20 minutes.

4.   Remelt the chocolate in the microwave if necessary, then spoon 1 teaspoon of the melted chocolate over the peanut butter layer in each

cup. Smooth the chocolate with the back of the spoon. Insert the points of two chocolate chips into the top of each peanut butter cup to make the bear's ears. Refrigerate until set, about 20 minutes.

5.   Gently remove the peanut butter cups from the cupcake liners.

6.   DECORATE THE PEANUT BUTTER CUPS: Place the melted white candy coating in a small plastic zip-top bag and cut off a small tip. Pipe on an oval for the bear muzzle with the white candy coating.

7.   Place the melted black and pink candy coatings in small plastic zip-top bags and cut off tiny tips. Pipe on the details for the eyes and mouth using the black candy coating, pipe cheeks using the pink candy coating. Serve immediately, or store in an airtight container and refrigerate until ready to serve.

CANDY & OTHER SWEETS

TEMPLATES

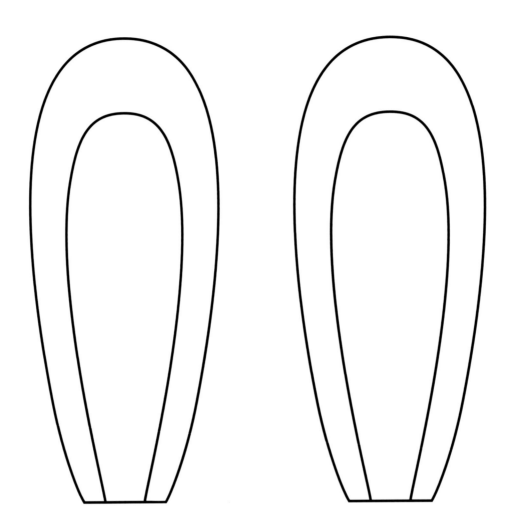

BUNNY CARROT CAKE

(PAGE 59)

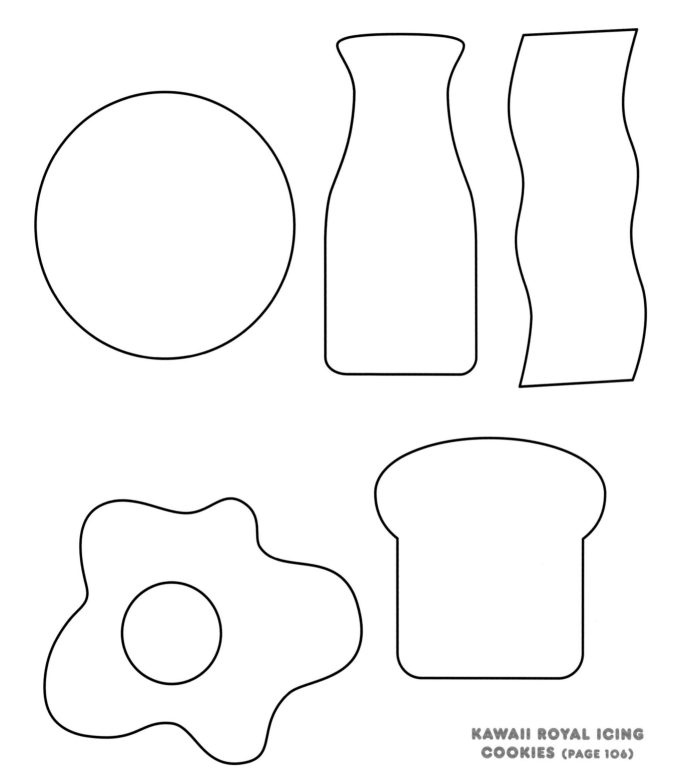

**KAWAII ROYAL ICING
COOKIES (PAGE 106)**

TEMPLATES

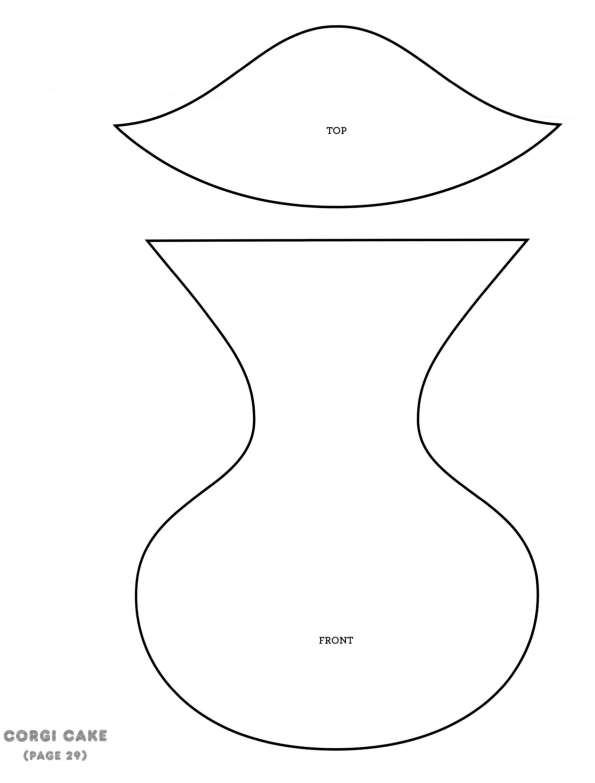

TOP

FRONT

CORGI CAKE
(PAGE 29)

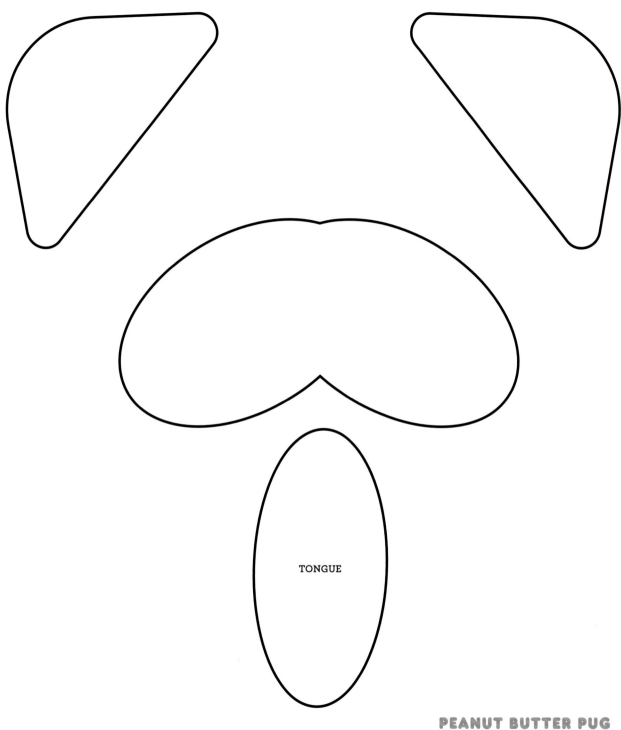

TONGUE

PEANUT BUTTER PUG PIE (PAGE 125)

JACK-O-LANTERN
PUMPKIN PIE (PAGE 127)

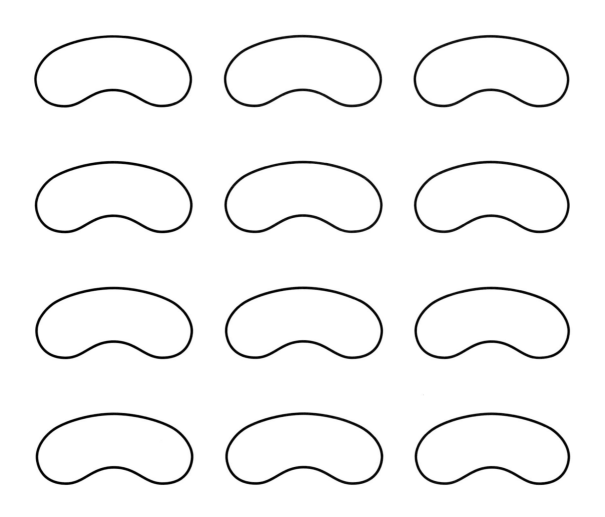

ACKNOWLEDGMENTS

Writing a cookbook during my freshman and sophomore year of college was a crazy, exciting, challenging, and (best of all) very sweet adventure, and I couldn't have done it without these amazing people in my life.

First of all, Mom and Dad, I love you so much! I'm forever grateful for all your genuine unconditional support in everything I've done. I know you insist that I've always been very independent, but I truly believe that your encouragement of me to chase after my goals is what led me to my dream life as a cookbook-writing Stanford student. I think you each deserve an individual and big, big thank-you for being the best parents I could ask for.

Mom, where would I be without you? Thank you not only for being an amazing, loving parent, but also for inspiring me to always be creative. Many of my favorite childhood memories come from our weekend shopping trips to craft stores, always on the lookout for something new to create. I think many of my successes are fueled by your enthusiasm and support for anything and everything I've been passionate about. Thank you for getting excited about my ideas and goals with me—it means so much more to me than you know! You inspire me with your thoughtfulness, kindness, and creativity, and I know that no acknowledgment is long enough to express how grateful I am for you.

Dad, thank you for being the number one taste-tester for the *Kawaii Sweet World* cookbook! And of course, thank you for all the love and support through-out my life as well. :-) I feel incredibly fortunate to have a dad who not only encourages me to follow my passions but also truly believes I will succeed in making my dreams a reality. Thank you for all the ways you've shown your support throughout my life: from learning how to put my hair into a bun for ballet class in elementary school to driving me to volunteer events in high school and now to reassuring me that no matter what I study, I will be successful as long as I'm driven and passionate about what I do in college. And while I may have learned to bake from Mom, I know I inherited my massive sweet tooth from you. Here's to many more years of always asking to see the dessert menu!

To my older brother, Chris, thank you for being my best friend growing up and for your genuine, caring, and supportive attitude. Whenever I've had a long day juggling schoolwork and "Kawaii Sweet World," I appreciate you being around to help calm me down and give advice. I cherish the memories of us baking snickerdoodles together and talking for hours late at night during high school about academics, friends, life, and more. I owe you red velvet cupcakes for life!

Thank you to my manager, Melissa Sun, for believing that "Kawaii Sweet World" was so much bigger than a girl who made videos about making cute desserts and DIYs. Without you, I would never have thought a cookbook was possible. I love your go-getter attitude, and I know we'll be working on lots more exciting projects together in the future as well. Let's keep chasing after the next big goal!

To my book agent, Kate McKean, for guiding me through the entire publication process when I was nineteen years old and for believing in this project from the beginning. Your expertise and drive has been absolutely critical, and I feel so lucky that I've gotten to work with you throughout this journey.

To my editor, Amanda Englander, and her assistant, Gabrielle Van Tassel; designer, Jen Wang; production editor, Patricia Shaw; production manager, Jessica Heim; publicist, Erica Gelbard; marketer, Daniel Wikey; and the entire team at Penguin Random House, for your enthusiasm about *Kawaii Sweet World* and your hard work in making it happen.

To our amazingly talented photographer, Andria Lo. Every single day of the photo shoot, you never failed to impress me with your creativity and keen eye for capturing desserts that beyond exceeded my expectations of food photography. To our prop stylist, Gordon Deng—I've never seen someone so artfully arrange crumbs on a plate and adeptly scatter sprinkles with a fan brush! And to our photography assistant, Sherese, and the whole photography team. I had an absolute blast during the photo shoot, and I was so amazed by your creativity. Thank you for making those twelve-plus-hour days so much more fun!

To my friends at Stanford—thank you for being taste-testers and the best, most supportive and inspiring family away from home I could ask for. Joceline, Grace, Lauren, Jason, Nate, Yu Jin, and so many more. I love you guys! And, of course, to my school, Stanford University, for fostering my love of learning, connecting with new people, and enjoying 70 degree sunshine.

To my high school teachers who believed in me and gave me the education to chase my dreams and goals. A special thank-you to the following people: Mr. Mattix, my computer science teacher, who gave me the confidence and know-how to pursue a degree in engineering. Ms. Yu, my Mandarin teacher, who supported both my valiant attempt to learn Chinese and my YouTube channel. I'll never forget how you linked to "Kawaii Sweet World" on our classroom website! Mrs. Weverka, my English teacher, for teaching me to write and communicate my ideas effectively. I have so much respect for these educators in my life who taught me to enjoy learning—whether the field was computer science, Mandarin, English, or any other subject. I sincerely thank you, and I hope you know that your work as teachers does not go unappreciated.

And finally, to my subscribers. Thank you for supporting me and making my dreams come true! Growing up as a shy, introverted teenager with a sweet tooth and a YouTube channel, I never thought "Kawaii Sweet World" could grow so much. I love you all, and I hope this book serves as not only a recipe guide for whipping up adorable desserts but also a reminder that you can achieve anything you want if you put in the hard work, perseverance, and passion. If you ask me, that's the sweetest treat of all!

INDEX

Published in the United States by Clarkson Potter/
Publishers, an imprint of the Crown Publishing
Group, a division of Penguin Random House LLC,
New York.
crownpublishing.com
clarksonpotter.com

CLARKSON POTTER is a trademark and
POTTER with colophon is a registered trademark
of Penguin Random House LLC.

Library of Congress Cataloging-in-Publication Data
Names: Fong, Rachel, author. | Lo, Andria, photog-
    rapher.
Title: Kawaii sweet world : 75 yummy recipes for
    baking that's (almost) too cute to eat / Rachel
    Fong ; photographs by Andria Lo.
Description: First edition. | New York : Clarkson
    Potter/Publishers, [2019] | Includes index.
Identifiers: LCCN 2018045930 (print) | LCCN
    2018047151 (ebook) | ISBN 9780525575436 |
    ISBN 9780525575429 (hardcover)
Subjects: LCSH: Confectionery. | LCGFT: Cook-
    books.
Classification: LCC TX783 (ebook) | LCC TX783
    .F66 2019 (print) | DDC 641.86--dc23
LC record available at https://lccn.loc.
    gov/2018045930

ISBN 978-0-525-57542-9
Ebook ISBN 978-0-525-57543-6

Printed in China

Book design by Jen Wang
Cover photographs by Andria Lo

10 9 8 7 6 5 4 3 2 1

First Edition